# THE APOSTLES' CREED

# THE
# APOSTLES' CREED:

## ITS RELATION TO

## PRIMITIVE CHRISTIANITY

BY

## H. B. SWETE, D.D.

HON. LITT.D. DUBLIN ;
FELLOW OF GONVILLE AND CAIUS COLLEGE,
REGIUS PROFESSOR OF DIVINITY, CAMBRIDGE.

## THIRD EDITION.

Cambridge:
AT THE UNIVERSITY PRESS.
1899

CAMBRIDGE UNIVERSITY PRESS
Cambridge, New York, Melbourne, Madrid, Cape Town, Singapore,
São Paulo, Delhi, Dubai, Tokyo, Mexico City

Cambridge University Press
The Edinburgh Building, Cambridge CB2 8RU, UK

Published in the United States of America by Cambridge University Press, New York

www.cambridge.org
Information on this title: www.cambridge.org/9780521170710

First paperback edition 2010

*A catalogue record for this publication is available from the British Library*

ISBN 978-0-521-17071-0 Paperback

THE following pages contain the substance of a short course of lectures which was delivered in the Divinity School at Cambridge during the Lent Term of the present year.

Their purpose is to enable educated members of the English Church who do not possess the leisure or the opportunities necessary for a fuller study of the subject to form some judgement upon a recent controversy which intimately concerns all who have been baptized into the Faith of the Apostles' Creed.

CAMBRIDGE,
*June,* 1894.

The second edition of this little book is a reprint of the first with the exception of a few changes in the notes suggested by the kindness of friends.

*October,* 1894.

In revising these pages for the press, use has been made of an advanced copy of Mr A. E. Burn's *Introduction to the Creeds,* supplied by the kindness of the author. References to Hahn's *Bibliothek der Symbole* have been conformed to the paging of the third edition of that work (Breslau, 1897). A few forms have been added to the collection of Creeds in the Appendix.

*January,* 1899.

# CONTENTS.

Μαθητεύσατε πάντα τὰ ἔθνη, βαπτίζοντες αὐτοὺς εἰς τὸ ὄνομα τοῦ πατρὸς καὶ τοῦ υἱοῦ καὶ τοῦ ἁγίου πνεύματος.

Ἀνάγκην ἔσχον γράψαι ὑμῖν παρακαλῶν ἐπαγωνίζεσθαι τῇ ἅπαξ παραδοθείσῃ τοῖς ἁγίοις πίστει.

# I.

No Christian document outside the limits of the Canon appeals to the loyalty of religious Englishmen so forcibly as the Apostles' Creed. For nearly three centuries and a half it has held its place in the Book of Common Prayer as the Creed of Baptism, of the Catechism, and of the daily offices. Even in the middle ages it was known to a relatively large number of the English laity through the instructions of the Clergy and the versions circulated in Primers. The English Reformers inherited a reverent esteem for the *Credo*, and gave it in their new Order of 1549 a place of honour equal to that which it had held in the Breviary and the Manual. From Prime it passed into Mattins, from Compline into Evensong; in the Baptismal office it was ordered to be rehearsed by minister and sponsors as in the Sarum *ordo ad faciendum catechumenum*, and sponsors were required as heretofore to provide for its being taught to their Godchildren. In the new Catechism the English Creed was printed in full, and the translation which appears there was afterwards adopted in the offices. It seems to be due to the Reformers themselves, probably to Cranmer, for while differing materially from the versions which are found in the Primers, it bears a close resemblance to the Creed set forth in the 'King's Book' of 1543, a work with which

the Archbishop was concerned[1]. Thus the English
Reformers gave the fullest sanction to the existing
Creed of the Western Church, and retained it in its old
position. They did more, for they enlarged the old
interrogative Creed of Baptism in such wise as to make
it practically identical with the Apostles' Creed. The
Church had perhaps from the first used at the font a
Creed shorter than that which she delivered to her
catechumens before their baptism. But the short interrogative Creed had gradually been enlarged in the
West by the introduction of clauses from the *symbolum*,
as may be seen by any one who will compare the Sarum
interrogatories with those of the Gelasian Sacramentary[2].
The English Reformers completed this process in 1549,
and, as a result, they were able to identify the Creed
professed at the font with that which is taught to the
baptized; in the Catechism the child is made to repeat
the Apostles' Creed as the Creed in which his sponsors
promised belief[3].

[1] *Formularies of the faith*, &c.
(Oxf. 1825), p. 226. The following
are the only variants: *Jesu, Ponce
Pilate, and* descended, *and* the third
day, *from death*. A similar form
appears in the Primer of 1545, and
in a paper left by Cranmer (*Works*,
ed. Parker Soc., ii. p. 83), with a
note, "The *Credo* I have trans-
lated."

[2] The Sarum Creed adds (1) *creatorem caeli et terrae*, (2) *catholicam*,
(3) *sanctorum communionem*, (4) *et
uitam aeternam post mortem*. Of
these (1), (2) and part of (4) are in
the Rheinau MS. of the 'Gelasian'
Sacramentary, which was written in
the eighth century and under Gallican influences (Wilson, *Gel. Sacr.*
pp. xxxiv—xxxv, 86—7), while (3)
occurs in a Bodleian MS. "which

may be assigned to a date near the
end of the ninth century"; but all
are wanting in the Vatican MS.,
which, notwithstanding the presence
of Gallican elements, seems to rest,
so far as regards the services from
Christmas to Pentecost, upon a
Roman Sacramentary of early date
(Wilson, p. xxvii).

[3] This is clearly implied in the
words of the Catechism, *They did
promise and vow...that I should believe all the articles of the Christian
faith...Dost thou not think that thou
art bound to believe...as they have
promised for thee?...Yes, verily...
Rehearse the articles of thy belief:*
upon which the child repeats the
Apostles' Creed as it now stands in
the Order for Morning and Evening
Prayer.

Thus in the Church of England since the publication of the first Prayer-book the Apostles' Creed has occupied a position even more important than that which it held in the mediaeval Church or now holds in Churches subject to the Roman See. Apart from all questions relating to the origin and history of the Creed, it commended itself to the practical instincts of the English Reformers as a sober and convenient summary of Christian belief. With the legend which attributed it to the Apostles they did not concern themselves. Nowell's catechism allows the alternative views that it "was first received from the Apostles' own mouth, or most faithfully gathered out of their writings." The latter explanation of the title was more in harmony with the way of thinking which prevailed at the time. An anonymous tract printed in 1548, and by some attributed to Cranmer, complains bitterly that the legend was still taught by the parish-priests as a necessary truth, "whereas it is at the best uncertain." It is a significant circumstance that in the first Prayer-book the document is simply called 'the Creed' without further description. The Articles of 1552 ruled that it was to be retained on the ground of its close agreement with Apostolic teaching; whatever its history, it could be proved by "most certayne warrauntes of holye Scripture."

A more critical method of study has led our own age to examine with minute care the sources and the interpretation of authoritative documents. With this examination there has come the challenge to reconsider the decision of the Reformers in reference to the Apostles' Creed. In England the dissatisfaction is at present limited to a section of the Nonconformists who

either regard all Creeds with aversion, or find themselves
unable to accept certain statements in this particular
formulary. In Germany recent controversy has been
more thoroughgoing, turning upon the history of
the Creed. There are indications that public attention
amongst ourselves will shortly be directed to the latter
point. Professor Harnack's pamphlet, which in Germany
passed through five-and-twenty editions during the
course of a year[1], has been reproduced in the pages of an
English periodical with a commendatory preamble from
the pen of the authoress of *Robert Elsmere*[2]. Most of its
facts are familiar to students of theology, as the learned
author fully recognises; but to many educated laymen
in England as well as in Germany they probably wear
the appearance of startling novelty, and the general
effect cannot fail to be for the time unsettling to those
who had regarded the Apostles' Creed as a document
uniformly primitive in its origin and teaching. But
Professor Harnack does not confine himself to the
history of his subject, in which he is a master; his
pamphlet abounds in statements upon matters of opinion
which the narrow limits of a popular discussion do not
permit him to support by argument, but which carry
with them the weight of a name deservedly high in
the estimation of educated Europe. The appearance
of his work in an English form becomes, therefore,
under present circumstances matter of grave concern
to those who are charged with the teaching of Christian

[1] *Das apostolische Glaubensbe-
kenntniss:* ein geschichtlicher Be-
richt nebst einem Nachwort. Von
D. Adolf Harnack, o. Professor der
Theologie an der Universität Berlin.
Berlin, 1892.

[2] *Nineteenth Century*, July, 1893,
art. xiv: "The Apostles' Creed by
Professor Harnack (with an Introduction by Mrs Humphry Ward)."
In the following pages Prof. Harnack's work has, for the sake of
convenience, been cited in Mrs H.
Ward's translation.

doctrine as it is maintained in the English Church. In the following pages I have not hesitated to take up the challenge which has been dropt, not by Dr Harnack himself, but by his English translator. Dr Harnack's remarks were addressed to the Protestant communions of Germany, and in their original form called for no discussion at the hands of members of the English Church. But their reproduction by an English writer in a popular form has transferred the controversy to English soil and thrown upon English Churchmen the duty of defending, if it be defensible, the Creed which the Edwardine Reformers inherited from the mediaeval Church.

The *symbolum Apostolorum* in mediaeval England was practically identical with that which we repeat to-day. A few variations have been collected by Dr Heurtley from the English versions of the Creed[1], but all the forms, English and Latin, clearly belong to one type. It is otherwise when we go back behind the Norman Conquest. In the British Museum there are two MSS. containing Creeds, one Latin, the other Greek[2], which fall short of the complete Apostles' Creed in a number of important particulars. These MSS. belong, it is stated, to the eighth and ninth centuries respectively, and are both apparently of English origin. Further, they present nearly the same text, and their text agrees very closely with the Roman Creed of the fourth century as it is represented in the Greek confession of Marcellus, and in the Latin of Rufinus. It seems, then,

---

[1] Heurtley, *Harm. Symb.*, p. 101 f.
[2] Heurtley, p. 74 ff.; Swainson, *Nicene and Apostles' Creeds*, p. 161; cf. Hahn, *Bibl. der Symbole*, ed. 3 (1897), pp. 23, 28; Kattenbusch, *das apostol. Symbol* (Leipzig, 1894), p. 64 ff. The texts will be found in the Appendix.

that in England down to the ninth century, a shorter Creed was current which was substantially identical with the old Creed of the Roman Church, and was probably brought to England by the Roman missionaries. There is reason to think that at Rome itself the shorter Creed was still known in the time of Gregory the Great. The great Oxford MS. of the Acts (cod. Laudianus, E), which was written in Sardinia, or at least was in the hands of a Sardinian owner between the sixth and eighth centuries, contains the Creed in a similar form written at the end of the Codex by a hand of the sixth or seventh century[1]. But Sardinia was in constant communication with Rome, and Januarius, Bishop of Cagliari, appears among Pope Gregory's most frequent correspondents. It is true that by this time the Creed of Constantinople may have taken the place of the Roman Creed in the *traditio symboli*, as the Gelasian Sacramentary seems to shew[2]; but the local Creed must have survived as a form of instruction after its deposition from liturgical honours, and as such would probably have found its way with Augustine into Kent. This simpler and briefer Creed, which is known to have been in use at Rome during the fourth century, may with great probability be carried back to the second. "We may regard it," Professor Harnack writes, "as an assured result of research that the Old Roman Creed...came into existence about or shortly before the middle of the second century."

The other recension, now known as the Apostles' Creed, is of later and not exclusively Roman origin[3].

---

[1] Heurtley, p. 60 ff. Comp. Gregory, *prolegg. in N. T.*, p. 411 sqq.

[2] Wilson, p. 53 ff.

[3] This longer form has usually been regarded as Gallican or Ger-

Traces of it may be seen in English episcopal professions of the ninth century[1], and it is found with an interlinear translation in a Lambeth MS. of the same period[2]. This fuller Creed had reached Ireland, whether in its completeness or not, before the end of the seventh century, for it has left distinct marks of its presence in the Creed of the Bangor Antiphonary[3]. To England it probably came quite a century later, not from Rome, but from the court of Charles, possibly through the hands of Alcuin. At all events it was here about A.D. 850 and existed for a while side by side with the Old Roman Creed, until official recognition secured for it an exclusive place in Psalters and books of devotion. After the beginning of the tenth century the older form ceases to appear in MSS. of English origin; and for a thousand years the later recension has held undisputed possession as the Baptismal Creed of the Church of England.

Thus the present Apostles' Creed is a document of composite origin with a long and complicated history. The basis of this document, the local Creed of the early Church of Rome, is substantially a product of the second century. But the Churches which derived their faith from Rome, or acknowledged the primacy of the Roman See, felt themselves under no obligation to adhere to the letter of the Roman Creed; and it received

man, and it is certain that most of its characteristic features appear for the first time in Gallican writers. Mr Burn, however (*Introduction to the Creeds*, p. 230 ff.) produces reasons for believing that the expansion of the Creed was accepted at Rome before the end of the 7th century.

[1] Swainson, p. 286, *n*. E.g. Diorlaf's profession (c. A.D. 860) has the

clauses *conceptum de Spiritu Sancto et natum ex Maria uirgine; ad inferos descendentem*.

[2] Heurtley, p. 88 ff.

[3] Warren, *Antiphonary of Bangor*, f. 19: *conceptum de Spiritu Sancto, natum de Maria uirgine, discendit ad inferos, sanctorum commonionem*, are in the Bangor form. "The date was A.D. 680—691" (Warren, p. viii). See Appendix.

at their hands not only verbal changes, but important
additions, involving in some cases new articles of belief.
The process was gradual, and some of the new clauses
do not appear before the sixth century, whilst others are
as late as the seventh.    The question arises whether
these accretions are of equal authority with the original
draft.    From the second century to the seventh is a far
cry, and in the interval the primitive teaching had been
obscured in some quarters by modifications and exten-
sions which do not now command general assent.    Do
the later clauses of the Apostles' Creed, or does any one
of them, fall under this category?

Let us place the two forms of the Creed side by side
for the purpose of comparison, italicising the later words
and clauses in the Apostles' Creed.

| ROMAN CREED. | APOSTLES' CREED. |
|---|---|
| Credo in Deum Patrem[1] omnipo-<br>tentem. | Credo in Deum Patrem omnipo-<br>tentem,<br>*creatorem caeli et terrae.* |
| Et in Christum Iesum unicum Fi-<br>lium eius, dominum nostrum,<br>qui natus est de Spiritu Sancto<br>ex Maria uirgine,<br>crucifixus sub Pontio Pilato et<br>sepultus, | Et in Iesum Christum Filium eius<br>unicum, dominum nostrum,<br>qui *conceptus* est de Spiritu Sancto,<br>natus ex Maria uirgine,<br>*passus* sub Pontio Pilato, cruci-<br>fixus, *mortuus* et sepultus,<br>*descendit ad inferna,* |
| tertia die resurrexit a mortuis,<br>ascendit in caelos, sedet ad dex-<br>teram Patris,<br>inde uenturus est iudicare uiuos<br>et mortuos. | tertia die resurrexit a mortuis,<br>ascendit *ad* caelos, sedet ad dex-<br>teram *Dei* Patris *omnipotentis;*<br>inde uenturus est iudicare uiuos<br>et mortuos. |
| Et in Spiritum Sanctum, sanctam<br>ecclesiam, remissionem pecca-<br>torum, carnis resurrectionem. | *Credo* in Spiritum Sanctum, sanctam<br>ecclesiam *catholicam, sanctorum<br>communionem,* remissionem pec-<br>catorum, carnis resurrectionem,<br>*uitam aeternam.* |

---

[1] Rufinus writes *Deo Patre,* &c., but Marcellus εἰς θεόν, and so the other early
forms.    *Unum* or *unicum* may have stood originally before *Deum* ; cf. Burn, *Introduction,* pp. 55 f., 58 ff.    On *Patrem* see below, p. 19 f.

It will be seen that much of the new matter in the later form consists of amplifications which either do not seriously affect the sense, or cannot be regarded as departures from primitive belief. *Creatorem caeli et terrae, uitam aeternam*, are additions of which no Christian can complain. *Conceptus, passus, mortuus*, supply new details which scarcely alter the balance of truth. Three points only need separate discussion : the clauses which affirm our Lord's Descent into Hell and the Communion of Saints, and the epithet 'Catholic' applied to the Holy Church.

But the doubts which are suggested by Professor Harnack's pamphlet reach much further. He contends that even the earliest form of the Roman Creed contained articles of belief in excess of the Apostolic teaching. Moreover, he suspects the interpretations that later generations of Christians have put upon articles which are confessedly primitive. Under the former of these counts he challenges the article which asserts the Miraculous Conception of the Lord, and that which confesses the Resurrection of 'the Flesh.' Under the latter he takes exception to the received explanation of the Names 'Father,' 'Only Son,' 'Holy Ghost,' regarding the doctrine of the hypostatic Trinity as one which lies entirely outside the original drift and meaning of the Creed.

It is evident that these criticisms tend largely to discredit the ancient Creed of Western Christendom. Their author, it is true, abstains from drawing any inference adverse to the retention of the Apostles' Creed by his own communion, and gracefully acknowledges the benefits which the early Roman Church has conferred upon Western Christians by transmitting so

precious an heirloom.    Nevertheless, if his conclusions
are sound, the fate of the Creed in many of the Reformed
Churches cannot be doubtful.    Nor is the Creed alone
in danger; articles of faith which are common to the
Reformed Churches and to those which are still subject
to the See of Rome, must stand or fall with it.    It is
difficult to exaggerate the gravity of these issues.

In the following passages an attempt will be made
to submit Professor Harnack's conclusions to a detailed
examination.    But instead of following him through
successive articles of the Creed, we propose to arrange
the points in dispute under three heads.    The strictly
theological articles will come first under review; then
those which recite the Evangelical history; lastly, those
which set forth the Doctrine of the Church.

## II.

*CREDO in Deum Patrem omnipotentem...et in Iesum Christum unicum Filium eius...et in Spiritum Sanctum.* The theology of the Creed forms its framework. The three articles just cited are distinguished from the rest by the fresh act of faith with which each is introduced (*credo in...et in...et in*). Thus the Baptismal Creed is seen to rest upon the Baptismal words. It was the answer of the Church to the Lord's final revelation of the Name of God. "As we are baptized, so (writes St Basil) must we believe[1]."

The theology of the Apostles' Creed starts with the confession of a Divine Fatherhood. It may be open to doubt whether this truth was directly recognised in the earliest form of the Roman Creed. Marcellus begins, 'I believe in God Almighty,' and Tertullian's statements of the Rule of Faith exhibit the same omission. Yet 'Patrem' stood in the Creed as it was known to Novatian and to Cyprian, and the Acts of Perpetua[2] seem to give it a place in the African Creed of the

---

[1] *ep.* 125 δεῖ γὰρ ἡμᾶς βαπτί-ζεσθαι μὲν ὡς παρελάβομεν, πιστεύειν δὲ ὡς βαπτιζόμεθα.

[2] *pass. S. Perpetuae* (ed. Robinson, p. 94) "omnipotentem Deum Patrem et Filium eius Iesum Christum Do-minum nostrum." The Greek gives another turn to the sentence, changing the reference to the Creed into a doxology of the Eastern type: δόξαν ἀνεπέμπομεν τῷ πατρὶ τῶν αἰώνων ἅμα τῷ μονογενεῖ αὐτοῦ υἱῷ, κ.τ.λ.

writer, who has been thought to be Tertullian himself.
It is fair then to assume that the word established itself
in symbolical use before the end of the second century.

But Harnack warns us that when the second century
professed its faith in God the Father, it did not necessarily attach to that name the significance which it
bore upon the lips of Christ and in the Epistles of
St Paul. The name itself is not common in the
Christian literature of the time, and when it is used,
it refers as a rule to the paternal relation of God to
the Creation. Therefore the author of the Creed " did
" not probably attribute the same meaning to the word
" as it bears in Matt. xi. 25 ff., Rom. viii. 15," although
" he does not stand in the way of such a meaning."

A creative paternity is ascribed to God in the New
Testament itself. He is the Father of "the lights"
of heaven (James i. 17) and of " the spirits " of men
(Heb. xii. 9); "we are also His offspring" (Acts xvii. 28) ;
" from Whom—the Father—every πατριά in heaven and
" on earth is named " (Eph. iii. 14, 15). The early post-
apostolic Church seized upon this conception and gave
it new prominence, for it supplied her with an answer
to Gnosticism, and a doctrine of God's relation to the
world which Paganism was half prepared to accept.
It appears in Clement of Rome : " Let us look (he
" writes) to the Father and Creator of the whole world[1]."
It is especially frequent, as we might expect, in the
early apologists. Christians are baptized, Justin tells
the pagan world, " in the Name of God the Father
" and Lord of the Universe, and of our Saviour Jesus
" Christ and the Holy Ghost[2]." " God is a Spirit,"

[1] 1 *Cor.* 19 τὸν πατέρα καὶ κτίστην :     καὶ δεσπότου θεοῦ: cf. 36, τοῦ δε-
cf. 35, ὁ δημιουργὸς καὶ πατήρ.     σπότου πάντων καὶ πατρός.
[2] *Ap.* 1. 61 τοῦ πατρὸς τῶν ὅλων

Tatian explains, "a Being Who, Himself invisible and "intangible, has become the Father of things sensible "and visible[1]." Theophilus states expressly that God is called Father, "because He existed before the Uni-"verse[2]."

Further, it is true that, as Harnack says, the Church of the second century laid special stress upon the sovereignty of God over the creation He has made. The conception of a supreme Lord (δεσπότης) is more frequent during this period than that of an universal Father. This conception, also, came from Scripture, perhaps chiefly from the Greek Old Testament. It occurs indeed in the New Testament, especially in passages which are coloured by Jewish ideas (Luke ii. 29, Acts iv. 24, 29, 2 Pet. ii. 1, Jude 4); but the post-apostolic Church probably received it from the LXX., where δεσπότης frequently represents אֲדֹנָי or even יְהֹוָה. In the Wisdom Books, for which the early Church entertained a high esteem, the word is specially used to denote the relation of the Creator to the Universe as its supreme Governor (Wisd. viii. 3, Sir. xxxvi. 1); "Lord of all creation" appears in 3 Macc. ii. 2 as a recognised form of invocation[3]. The Church took over the conception from the Synagogue, and there was abundant reason why in her first struggles with the world she should rejoice in a truth which reminded her where her strength lay. The Creed reflects this truth in the word 'Almighty,' for *omnipotens* is παντοκράτωρ rather than παντοδύναμος, not so much the 'Almighty'

---

[1] *Or. c. Graec.* 4 ἀόρατός τε καὶ ἀναφής, αἰσθητῶν καὶ ὁρατῶν αὐτὸς γεγονὼς πατήρ.

[2] *ad Autol.* i. 4 διὰ τὸ εἶναι αὐτὸν πρὸ τῶν ὅλων.

[3] Sap. viii. 3 ὁ πάντων δεσπότης. Sir. xxxvi. 1 δέσποτα ὁ θεὸς πάντων: 3 Macc. ii. 2 δέσποτα πάσης κτίσεως: cf. 2 Macc. xiii. 14.

as the 'All-Ruler[1].' It is therefore quite possible and even probable that the combination *Pater Omnipotens* points in the first instance to the relation of God to the world which He has created, and over which He exercises sovereign rights, and Harnack has done good service by directing attention to an aspect of the words which was certainly primitive, but in these days is too often left out of sight.

But the question remains whether this aspect of the Divine Paternity, which circumstances placed foremost in the thought of the second century, was allowed to overshadow the deeper revelation of the Baptismal Words. As a matter of fact, the early Christian writers who speak of God's fatherly relation to Nature, speak also of His special relation to Jesus Christ and to the members of the Church. " Let us approach Him "(Clement exhorts) in holiness of soul, lifting up to " Him pure hands and undefiled, loving our gentle and " compassionate Father, who made us an elect portion

---

[1] Παντοκράτωρ stands in the Eastern Creeds regularly, and the combination πατὴρ παντοκράτωρ is frequent in documents of the second and third centuries (cf. Gebhardt and Harnack, *patr. app.* I. ii. p. 134). In Greek versions of the Roman Creed, from Marcellus downwards, πατέρα παντοκράτορα is the rendering of *patrem omnipotentem ;* the only exception seems to be the late form printed by Hahn, p. 32, in which a Vatican MS. gives παντοδύναμον; the St Gall MS. 338 and the Corpus MS. 468 read ἐν δεξιᾷ θεοῦ πατρὸς [τοῦ] παντοδυνάμου in the second part of the Creed, but retain παντοκράτορα in the first article. Παντοδύναμος occurs but rarely in the O. T. (only in Sap. vii. 23, xi. 18, xviii. 15), whereas παντοκράτωρ is the equivalent of צְבָאוֹת in some eighty instances. *Omnipotens* is the O. L. rendering of παντοκράτωρ in 2 Kings vii. 8, 27, 3 Kings xix. 10, Jer. iii. 19, &c. For the meaning of παντοκράτωρ cf. Theoph. *ad Autol.* i. 4 παντοκράτωρ, ὅτι αὐτὸς τὰ πάντα κρατεῖ. Cyril, *cat.* 8 π. ἐστὶν ὁ πάντων κρατῶν, ὁ πάντων ἐξουσιάζων. A later age undoubtedly understood *omnipotens* in the Creed as = παντοδύναμος; cf. Aug. *de symb. ad catech.*: facit quidquid uult: ipsa est omnipotentia...nemo resistit omnipotenti. But the writers of the Old Roman Creed probably followed the leading of the Greek word which represented the Father as Sovereign of the Universe. See, however, Caspari, *Quellen*, II. pp. 92, 208 ff.

"(ἐκλογῆς μέρος) for Himself" (c. 29). The homily known as the Second Epistle of Clement, a survival from the second century, possibly of Roman origin[1], abounds in references to the Father, and identifies Him with the Father of Christ (c. 3) and the Father of Christians (cc. 10, 14)[2]. Ignatius dwells almost exclusively on His relation to our Lord, quite after the manner of St Paul (*Eph.* 5, *Magn.* 1, 3, 7, 8). In Hermas, whose practice is specially significant as that of a Roman Christian who, according to the commonly accepted view, belonged to the very generation which gave shape to the Roman Creed, God is called Father only in His relation to the Son and to the Church (*uis.* iii. 9. 10 ; *sim.* v. 6. 3, 4 ; ix. 12. 2)[3]. The Apologists, addressing the heathen, led them to identify the Father of the Universe with the Father of Christ. "The Almighty Creator of all things," writes the unknown author of the Epistle to Diognetus, "sent His Son as a King might send a Royal Prince, "as sending God[4]." "Jesus Christ," says Justin, "is "the begotten Son of God after a manner peculiar to "Himself[5]."

In the face of these facts it is arbitrary to say that the deeper sense of the word was probably absent from the mind of the author of the Creed. It is more than arbitrary in view of the words that immediately follow in the Creed itself : *et in Christum Iesum unicum Filium eius.* Can it be believed that *Patrem* in the first clause of the Creed has no prospective reference to *Filium* in

---

[1] Cf. Harnack, *Chronol.*, p. 438 ff.

[2] Ps. Clement. 2 *Cor.* 3 ἔγνωμεν δι' αὐτοῦ τὸν πατέρα τῆς ἀληθείας...λέγει δὲ καὶ αὐτός Τὸν ὁμολογήσαντά με ὁμολογήσω αὐτὸν ἐνώπιον τοῦ πατρός μου. § 15 ποιοῦντες τὸ θέλημα τοῦ πατρὸς ἡμῶν θεοῦ.

[3] See the note in Gebhardt and Harnack on *uis.* l.c.

[4] *ad Diogn.* 7 ὡς βασιλεὺς πέμπων υἱὸν βασιλέα ἔπεμψεν, ὡς θεὸν (? ὡς θεὸς θεὸν) ἔπεμψεν.

[5] *Ap.* i. 22 μόνος ἰδίως υἱὸς τῷ θεῷ γεγέννηται: cf. *ib.* 13, 14, 65.

the second ?  Rufinus's explanation cannot be entirely
wrong, " Fili intellige Patrem[1]"; or Cyril's, Τῷ εἰπεῖν
ὅτι πατήρ, ἤδη ἐδηλώσαμεν ὅτι καὶ υἱὸν ἔχει[2].  The fourth
century may have insisted on this aspect of the truth too
exclusively, but the second did not overlook it.


Passing to the second article of the Creed, we are
invited to enquire in what sense Jesus Christ is confessed
to be the "only Son" of God.

*Et in Christum Iesum unicum Filium eius*: so runs
the Roman Creed of the fourth century as attested by
both Marcellus and Rufinus ; so too the other Italian
forms of the Roman Creed, e.g. those of Milan, Turin,
Aquileia, Ravenna, and the later forms prevalent in
Spain, Gaul, Ireland, and England[3].  *Unicum*, however,
appears to have been wanting in African types of the
Creed ; it is not in Tertullian's accounts of the Rule of
Faith, or in the Creeds of Cyprian and Augustine.
Even Novatian of Rome omits it, and, at a later
time, Nicetas.  Thus, although possibly present in the
Roman Creed before the end of the second century,
it cannot claim to have been universally admitted by
the Western Churches.  But, as Harnack points out,
the matter is not of serious moment, for *unicum* adds
nothing to the sense ; He who is confessed to be ' the
' Son' of God must needs be the ' Only Son.'  It is only
as authoritatively interpreting *Filium* that *unicum* is
important.

[1] Rufin. *in Symb.* 4.  He adds:
sicut enim nemo dicitur 'dominus,'
nisi habeat uel possessionem uel
seruum cui dominetur ; ita et 'pater'
nullo pacto quis dici potest nisi filium
habens.  hoc igitur ipso nomine quo
Deus Pater appellatur, cum Patre
pariter subsistere etiam Filius de-
monstratur,

[2] Cyril *cat.* 8.

[3] The only variation is in the
order of the words *Christum Iesum*.

There can be no doubt that *unicum* (for which *unigenitum* is occasionally substituted) represents τὸν μονογενῆ, which answers to it in the Creed of Marcellus. Tertullian indeed has "unicum Deum omnipotentem[1]" for ἕνα θεὸν παντοκράτορα, so that if *unicum* in the Roman Creed had stood before *Christum*, we might have understood it in the sense of *unum*. But *unicum Filium* points quite certainly either to Gen. xxii. 2[2], where the Old Latin version, as given by Cyprian, renders "Accipe filium tuum unicum," or to the Gospel of St John; the latter being more probably the immediate source. St John's phrase finds indeed no place in subapostolic writers, though Ignatius approaches to it when he calls our Lord the Only Son (τοῦ μόνου υἱοῦ)[3]. It seems to have been first seized upon by the Valentinians, who gave the name Monogenes to the Aeon Nous. The Catholic writers began, although slowly, to reclaim it; Justin uses it sparingly; it occurs once in the Smyrnaean circular on the martyrdom of Polycarp; in Irenaeus at length it becomes frequent. Thus it is not unlikely that the word took its place in the vocabulary of the Church by way of protest against the Valentinian misuse of St John; and the same cause may have gained for it admission to the Creed. Valentinus taught at Rome during the episcopates of Hyginus, Pius, and Anicetus, i.e. between 140 and 160 A.D.—the very epoch to which the making of the Creed is assumed to belong. The Valentinians, or at least the Anatolic School, distinguished Monogenes from the historical manifestation,

---

[1] *de uel. uirg.* 1 (cf. *adu. Prax.* 2).

[2] LXX. λάβε τὸν υἱόν σου τὸν ἀγαπητόν. Aquila seems to have rendered יְחִיד here by μονογενής, and the word must have stood in

"at least some form of the LXX." (Hort, *Two Dissertations*, p. 49, *n.*).

[3] Gebhardt and Harnack, *patr. app.* I. ii. p. 136.

remarking that St John guards himself by writing "we "beheld His glory, glory as of the only-begotten," where the qualifying word *as* bars out complete identification[1]. If the Church of Rome admitted the word under these circumstances, it can hardly have done so except by way of an answer to the Valentinian interpretation. To confess faith in Jesus Christ as the only-begotten Son, was to identify the Only-begotten with the historical Person who was born and died and rose again.

Harnack however contends that when the Creed calls Jesus Christ 'the Son' or 'the only-begotten 'Son,' it does not claim for Him a preexistent Sonship, but limits its view to His Incarnate Life. "After "Nicaea these words came to be unanimously believed "by the Church to refer to the prehistoric and eternal "Sonship of Christ...But to transfer this conception to "the Creed is to transform it. It cannot be proved that "about the middle of the second century the idea 'only "'Son' was understood in this sense: on the contrary "the evidence of history conclusively shews that it was "not so understood."

There can be no doubt that the Valentinians recognised in the Monogenes of the Fourth Gospel a prehistoric Being, or that they were right in this exegesis. It is equally certain that when the Church began to use the word in reference to our Lord, she used it in this sense. "He was the Only Begotten of the "Father of the Universe," writes Justin, "inasmuch as He "was after a peculiar manner produced from the Father as

---

[1] Clem. Al. *exc.* § 7 ὁ μὲν μείνας μονογενὴς υἱὸς εἰς τὸν κόλπον τοῦ πατρὸς τὴν ἐνθύμησιν διὰ τῆς γνώσεως ἐξηγεῖται τοῖς αἰῶσιν, ὡς ἂν καὶ ὑπὸ τοῦ κόλπου αὐτοῦ προβληθείς· ὁ δὲ ἐνταῦθα ὀφθεὶς οὐκ ἔτι μονο- γενής, ἀλλ' ὡς μονογενὴς πρὸς τοῦ ἀποστόλου προσαγορεύεται· 'δόξαν ὡς μονογενοῦς'· ὅτι εἷς καὶ ὁ αὐτὸς ὢν ἐν μὲν τῇ κτίσει πρωτότοκός ἐστιν 'Ιησοῦς, ἐν δὲ τῷ πληρώματι μονο- γενής.

" His Word and Power[1]." Justin, like Valentinus, taught at Rome in days not far removed from those which witnessed the genesis of the Creed, and his conception of the sense of μονογενής may fairly be regarded as determining the meaning of the word in the Creed.

But if we limit our enquiry to the essential point, the nature of the Sonship assigned to our Lord by writers contemporary with the Creed or anterior to it, the evidence against Harnack's view becomes stronger. Behind Justin is Aristides, and his brief statement of the common faith includes the preexistence of the Son, " the Son of God most high is confessed...as having " come down from heaven[2]." Further back, we have the frequent references of Ignatius to a Sonship which lies beyond the limit of time. " Jesus Christ...came forth " from one Father " (*Magn.* 7); is " both of Mary and of " God " (*Eph.* 7), " of the family of David according to " the flesh, Son of God by [the Divine] Will and Power " (*Smyrn.* 1); " was with the Father before the world was " (*Magn.* 6). One remark of Ignatius seems indeed to conflict with our interpretation of his testimony. He contrasts (*Eph.* 7) the two natures in Christ in such a manner as to predicate generation of the manhood only ; the one Christ is both γεννητὸς καὶ ἀγέννητος, generate as Man, ingenerate in His Divine life[3]. This denial of a Divine generation characterises an early phase of Christian thought which associated with ' generation '

---

[1] *dial.* 105 μονογενὴς γὰρ ὅτι ἦν τῷ πατρὶ τῶν ὅλων οὗτος ἰδίως ἐξ αὐτοῦ λόγος καὶ δύναμις γεγεννημένος ...προεδήλωσα. Justin has just quoted Ps. xxi (=xxii). 19.

[2] *ap.* p. 110 (ed. Robinson) οὗτος δὲ ὁ υἱὸς τοῦ θεοῦ τοῦ ὑψίστου ὁμολογεῖται...ἀπ' οὐρανοῦ καταβάς, κ.τ.λ. Compare Hennecke, *die Apologie des*

*Aristides*, p. 9.

[3] The words form part of a series of contrasts : εἷς ἰατρός ἐστιν σαρκικὸς καὶ πνευματικός, γεννητὸς καὶ ἀγέννητος, ἐν ἀνθρώπῳ θεός, ἐν θανάτῳ ζωὴ ἀληθινή, καὶ ἐκ Μαρίας καὶ ἐκ θεοῦ, πρῶτον παθητὸς καὶ τότε ἀπαθής, Ἰησοῦς Χριστὸς ὁ κύριος ἡμῶν.

ideas inconsistent with the unchangeableness of God. The doctrine of an Eternal Generation was unknown to Ignatius, and any lower conception was felt to be unworthy of the Divine Essence. But to deny to the Eternal Logos a generation such as Ignatius had in view, was not to deny His prehistoric Sonship. The conception of a Divine Sonship was realised by the Church before the conception of a Divine generation, and Ignatius belonged to the earlier stage. "Sub-"stantially," as Dr Lightfoot shews, Ignatius "held the "same views as the Nicene fathers respecting the Person "of Christ[1]." He would probably have been startled by language which is freely used in pages of Justin and Tatian; it might have seemed to him precarious to speak of the Word as $\gamma\epsilon\nu\nu\eta\theta\epsilon\ifmmode\acute{\imath}\else\'{\i}\fi\varsigma$ or $\gamma\epsilon\nu\nu\acute{\omega}\mu\epsilon\nu\sigma\varsigma$; but he would surely have been roused to indignation had any teacher risen up to say that the Word was not already Son of God when He was with the Father, before He was made Man.

Professor Harnack brings to his study of subapostolic writers a preconception which to his own mind has assumed the dimensions of a historical fact. Primitive Christianity, as he conceives it, had two Christologies, the one pneumatic, the other adoptianist. The former regarded the Christ as a preexistent[2] Spirit who was made Man; the latter fixed its thoughts upon the historical Person who received from the Almighty Father a Sonship unique indeed and Divine but not essential. The former was the point of view adopted by such writers as Barnabas, Clement, the author of the Homily, Ignatius, Polycarp; the latter prevailed in

---

[1] *Apostolic Fathers*, pt. ii, vol. ii, p. 93.

[2] On Harnack's conception of the doctrine of the preexistence of Christ as held in the early Church see especially his *Dogmengeschichte*, ed. 2, I. p. 710 ff.

circles which were regarded by these writers as heretical. But the Christology which asserted the preexistence of our Lord did not connect His preexistence with a filial relation to God. It is in Hermas that the two systems are first fused together, and the Sonship is seen to have belonged to the preexistent Christ[1].

For our purpose it might suffice to point out that if the supposed fusion took place in Hermas, it was probably earlier than the formation of the Creed. But Harnack's theory rests on evidence which is quite inadequate. It is true that the preexistence of Christ was ignored or denied in certain quarters, and His Sonship limited to the human life, or that part of it which followed the Baptism. It is also true that the earliest orthodox writers spoke of the preexistent Christ as Spirit[2], and connected His Sonship more especially with the human life by which it was manifested[3]. Further, the Church had not yet learned to conceive of a Divine generation as involved in the fact of a Divine Sonship. All this is admitted. But it does not establish Dr Harnack's contention. Evidence has been produced to shew that about the middle of the third century a prehistoric and premundane Sonship was ascribed by the majority of believers to Jesus Christ. There is no sufficient evidence on the other hand that during any part of the second century the Sonship was limited by orthodox Christians to the manifestation of the Word in human flesh.

---

[1] *Lehrbuch der Dogmengeschichte*, i. p. 160 ff. *Grundriss der Dogmengeschichte*, p. 29 ff. (= E. T. p. 51).

[2] See e.g. Ps. Clem. 2 *Cor.* 9 Χριστὸς ὁ Κύριος…ὢν μὲν τὸ πρῶτον πνεῦμα ἐγένετο σάρξ, with Lightfoot's note.

[3] Comp. Justin, *dial.* 88 φωνὴ ἐκ τῶν οὐρανῶν ἅμα ἐληλύθει, ἥτις καὶ διὰ Δαβὶδ λεγομένη ὡς ἀπὸ προσώπου αὐτοῦ λέγοντος ὅπερ αὐτῷ ἀπὸ τοῦ πατρὸς ἔμελλε λέγεσθαι Υἱός μου εἶ σύ, ἐγὼ σήμερον γεγέννηκά σε· τότε γένεσιν αὐτοῦ λέγων γίνεσθαι τοῖς ἀνθρώποις ἐξ ὅτου ἡ γνῶσις αὐτοῦ ἔμελλε γίνεσθαι. Hippol. *c. Noet.* p. 54 (ed. Lagarde) οὔτε γὰρ ἄσαρκος καὶ καθ' ἑαυτὸν ὁ λόγος τέλειος ἦν υἱός, καίτοι τέλειος λόγος ὢν μονογενής.

# III.

AFTER reciting the facts of the Incarnate life, to
which we shall presently return, the Roman Creed
proceeds, *Et in Spiritum Sanctum,* "And [I believe] in
"the Holy Ghost." This clause opens the third division
of the Creed, and thus corresponds to the clauses which
confess the Father and the Son[1]; but whereas in the
first and second articles the name is followed by a
personal definition, the confession of the Holy Spirit
stands by itself, and the Creed passes on at once to
other articles of belief. A comparison of the 'Nicene'
Creed places this fact in a stronger light, for there the
Holy Ghost is declared to be τὸ κύριον, τὸ ζωοποιόν,
τὸ ἐκ τοῦ πατρὸς ἐκπορευόμενον, κ.τ.λ.; whilst the
Western Creed affirms nothing beyond His existence.
"It looks therefore," Professor Harnack says, "as though
"the writer of the Creed did not conceive the Holy Ghost
"as a Person, but as a Power and Gift. This is indeed
"literally the case. No proof can be shewn that about
"the middle of the second century the Holy Ghost was

---

[1] Rufin. *in Symb.* 35 ea quae in
superioribus paulo latius de Christo
sunt tradita...dum media intercedunt
personae ipsius coaptata Sancti
Spiritus commemorationem paulo
longius reddiderunt. ceterum si
solius diuinitatis ratio habeatur, eo
modo quo in principio dicitur *Credo
in Deo Patre omnipotente,* et post
haec *In Iesu Christo Filio eius unico
Domino nostro,* ita iungitur *Et in
Spiritu Sancto.*

"believed in as a Person. This conception, on the
"contrary, is one of much later date, which was still
"unknown to most Christians by the middle of the
"fourth century.... In the Creed the Holy Ghost is
"conceived of as a gift, but as a gift by which the Divine
"life is offered to the believer; for the Spirit of God
"is God Himself."

These words raise the whole question whether the
doctrine of the coexistence of three hypostases in
God was implicit in the faith of the second century.
Since even in the fourth century the terminology of the
doctrine was by no means fixed or uniform, no one will
expect to find in writers of the second century an
accurate use of such words as οὐσία, ὑπόστασις, πρόσωπον. It will suffice if we can shew that the sub-
apostolic age and that which succeeded to it were
conscious of a distinction between God and the Spirit
of God, analogous to that which was seen to exist
between God and the Logos.

Such a consciousness betrays itself in a Roman
document earlier than the Creed by perhaps half a
century. When Clement of Rome asks, "Have we not
"one God and one Christ and one Spirit of grace which
"was poured out upon us[1]?," whilst emphasising the historical manifestations of the Son and the Spirit, does he
not at once distinguish Them from God and from Each
Other, and yet coordinate the Three? When he permits
himself the use of the adjuration, "As God lives, and
"the Lord Jesus Christ lives, and the Holy Spirit, the
"faith and hope of the elect[2]," is it not fair to say that

---

[1] 1 *Cor.* 46. 6 οὐχὶ ἕνα θεὸν ἔχομεν καὶ ἕνα Χριστὸν καὶ ἓν πνεῦμα τῆς χάριτος τὸ ἐκχυθὲν ἐφ' ἡμᾶς;
[2] *ib.* 58. 2 ζῇ γὰρ ὁ θεὸς καὶ ζῇ ὁ κύριος Ἰησοῦς Χριστὸς καὶ τὸ πνεῦμα τὸ ἅγιον. For the form of adjuration cf. Serapion *ap.* Euseb. v. 19 ζῇ ὁ θεὸς ὁ ἐν τοῖς οὐρανοῖς.

he claims for the Son and the Spirit a personal Life which is not absolutely identified with the Life of the Father, and yet is understood to be Divine?

Yet there is reason to think that by the middle of the second century the Church had gained a firmer grasp upon the conception of the Spirit's personal distinctness than she possessed in the days of Clement. The growing use of the Fourth Gospel contributed to this result. Dr Harnack characteristically observes that this "cannot be shewn," but it can at least be made probable. The 'Paraclete' appears together with the 'Only-begotten' in the Valentinian system, whilst Montanism called the attention of the Catholic Church to the Johannine title. "They called him (Vettius "Epagathus) the Christian's advocate, and he had the "'Advocate' within him[1]." So wrote the Churches of Lyons and Vienne in A.D. 177. Tertullian gives the personal name a place in the Rule of Faith, and it is in the early Creed of Jerusalem, where it may have gained admission about the same period. But the free use of the masculine noun $\pi\alpha\rho\acute{\alpha}\kappa\lambda\eta\tau o\varsigma$ could hardly have failed to influence Christian thought. It did not originate the conception of the Spirit's distinct personality, for we have seen that that was already latent in the words of the Roman Clement; but it gave fuller and clearer expression to the belief. Thus the Passion of Perpetua, written under Montanist influence, discriminates quite unambiguously between the Person of the Spirit and His work: "uiderint qui unam uirtutem "Spiritus unius Sancti pro aetatibus iudicent temporum"; —"ut nouae quoque uirtutes unum et eundem semper "Spiritum Sanctum usque adhuc operari testificentur[2]."

---

[1] ap. Euseb. *H. E.* v. I.　　　[2] ed. Robinson, pp. 60, 94.

To Tertullian the Western Church owes the word *trinitas*, and although his Trinity is an 'economy,' i.e. is viewed chiefly in reference to the manifestation of God in human history, it is seen to be rooted in the inner life of the Godhead. The 'persons'—he uses the term—are *gradus, formae, species,* and are at once inseparable and distinct ("inseparatos ab alterutro..testor.. "dico alium esse Patrem et alium Filium et alium "Spiritum"); the Scriptures represent each Person as invested with a 'property' which is peculiar to Himself ("unamquamque personam in sua proprietate con- "stituunt"); the Second and Third Persons are derived from the First—the Second immediately, the Third through the medium of the Second[1]. If this teaching, which comes from the first quarter of the third century, falls short of the theology of the third quarter of the fourth century, it does so chiefly because Tertullian has not grasped the timelessness of the mutual relations of the Divine Life, or the truth that the Second and Third Persons receive from the First the whole essence of the Godhead. Origen carries us many steps nearer to the full evolution of the doctrine. Christian tradition, he says, has left certain points with regard to the Holy Ghost's manner of existence uncertain, yet it certainly places Him on an equality with the Father and the Son[2], and regards Him as possessing spiritual life. Indeed so far is Origen from ignoring the distinctness of the Holy Spirit[3], that he goes to the length of suggesting that the Spirit, since He is neither the Father nor

[1] *adu. Prax.* 2, 9, 11.
[2] *de princ.* i. *praef.* honore ac dignitate Patri ac Filio sociatum tradiderunt Spiritum Sanctum; in hoc non iam manifeste discernitur utrum natus an innatus uel Filius etiam Dei ipse habendus sit necne. Comp. Aug. *de fide et symb.* 19.
[3] *de princ.* i. 1. 4 Sp. S. subsistentia est intellectualis et proprie subsistit et exstat.

the Son, must be placed among the γενητά made by the Son[1]. He interprets Hab. iii. 2 (LXX., ἐν μέσῳ δύο ζώων γνωσθήσῃ) as referring to the Son and the Spirit[2]. In one place he directly distinguishes the χαρίσματα of the Spirit from the Person : " I think that "the Holy Spirit supplies the saints with the material "(if I may so speak) of the gifts that they receive from " God, this material finding hypostatic existence (ὑφε- " στώσης) in the Holy Spirit[3]." He realises more clearly than Tertullian that the Holy Spirit had no beginning of existence : " He would not have been reckoned in the " Unity of the Trinity together with the unchangeable " Father and the Son if He had not been always Holy " Spirit." He grasps the truth of His essential equality with the Father and the Son : " No relation in the " Trinity can be said to be greater or less[4]."

Arianism was in the first instance a protest against the Sabellian confusion of the Persons[5]. Arius spoke freely of three οὐσίαι or ὑποστάσεις[6]; and though in the long conflict that followed his condemnation the use of these terms was in some quarters abandoned or depre-

---

[1] *in Joann.* ii. 6.

[2] *de princ.* i. 3. 4.

[3] *in Joann. l.c.* οἶμαι δὲ τὸ ἅγιον πνεῦμα τὴν (ἵν' οὕτως εἴπω) ὕλην τῶν ἀπὸ θεοῦ χαρισμάτων παρέχειν τοῖς δι' αὐτὸ καὶ τὴν μετοχὴν αὐτοῦ χρηματίζουσιν 'ἁγίοις,' τῆς εἰρημένης ὕλης τῶν χαρισμάτων ἐνεργουμένης μὲν ἀπὸ τοῦ θεοῦ, διακονουμένης δὲ ὑπὸ τοῦ Χριστοῦ, ὑφεστώσης δὲ κατὰ τὸ ἅγιον πνεῦμα.

[4] *de princ.* i. 3. 4 nunquam utique in unitate Trinitatis, id est, Dei Patris inconuertibilis et Filii Eius etiam ipse Spiritus Sanctus haberetur, nisi quia et ipse semper erat Sp. S. *ib.* 7 nihil in Trinitate maius minusue dicendum est.

[5] Socr. *H. E.* 1. 5 Ἄρειος... οἰόμενος τὸ Σαβελλίου τοῦ Λίβυος δόγμα εἰσηγεῖσθαι τὸν ἐπίσκοπον, ἐκ φιλονεικίας κατὰ διάμετρον εἰς τὸ ἐναντίον τῆς τοῦ Λίβυος δόξης ἀπέκλινε.

[6] Ath. *or. c. Arian.* 1. 6 μεμερισμέναι τῇ φύσει καὶ ἀπεξενωμέναι καὶ ἀπεσχοινισμέναι καὶ ἀλλότριοι καὶ ἀμέτοχοί εἰσιν ἀλλήλων αἱ οὐσίαι τοῦ πατρὸς καὶ τοῦ υἱοῦ καὶ τοῦ ἁγίου πνεύματος, καὶ ὡς αὐτὸς ἐφθέγξατο, ἀνόμοιοι πάμπαν ἀλλήλων ταῖς τε οὐσίαις καὶ δόξαις εἰσὶν ἐπ' ἄπειρον. *de Syn.* 15 ἀνεπίμικτοι ἑαυταῖς εἰσιν αἱ ὑποστάσεις αὐτῶν. Comp. Gwatkin, *Studies of Arianism,* p. 27.

cated, no attempt was made to merge the personality of
the Spirit in that of the Father or of the Son. The first
Synod of Sirmium anathematises those who speak of the
Three as "one person" (ἓν πρόσωπον), or identify the
Holy Ghost with the Ingenerate God, or call Him a
part of the Father or of the Son; whilst on the other
hand it equally condemns a proposition which the
Catholics certainly did not support, that the Father, the
Son, and the Holy Spirit are three Gods[1]. From any
positive statements about the Person of the Spirit the
Arian Creeds usually abstain, contenting themselves
with expressing belief in His operations; but the title
Paraclete, which suggests personality, is used in these
documents with remarkable frequency. Thus the last
of the series (Constantinople, A.D. 360) confesses,
"And [we believe] in the Holy Ghost, which the Only-
"Begotten Son of God Himself, the Christ, our Lord
"and God, promised to send to mankind as Paraclete
"(according as it is written), the Spirit of Truth; which
"He sent to them when He went up to Heaven[2]."

We have now passed the middle of the fourth century,
when according to Harnack's view most Christians were
still ignorant of the personality of the Holy Ghost; yet
no trace of the assumed ignorance has met us hitherto.
Origen, indeed, refers to some who held that the Holy
Spirit was impersonal[3], and Jerome accuses Lactantius
of the same error: "Spiritus Sancti negat substantiam,
"et errore Iudaico dicit eum uel ad Patrem referri uel
"Filium, et sanctificationem utriusque personae sub eius
"nomine demonstrari[4]." But assuming that Jerome's

---

[1] Hahn, p. 199.
[2] *ib.* p. 209.
[3] ap. Corder. caten. in S. Ioann.,
p. 90: οὐ γάρ, ὥς τινες οἴονται, ἐνέρ-
γειά ἐστι θεοῦ, οὐκ ἔχον κατ' αὐτοὺς
ὑπάρξεως ἰδιότητα. I owe the reference to Mr Brooke.
[4] *ep. ad Pamm. et Ocean.* § 7.

charge is well founded, Lactantius is the solitary known champion within the Catholic Church of this "Jewish "error." It appears, however, to have been revived by certain members of the Macedonian party, who found themselves embarrassed by the question, 'If the Holy 'Ghost be not God, who or what is He?' The sounder thinkers and more reverent believers of the party shrank from calling Him a creature. Some fell back upon a confession of ignorance; others took the bolder course of representing the Holy Spirit as the Divine energy. The fact is mentioned by Gregory of Nazianzus, who describes adherents of this view as "some of our "Christian philosophers[1]." He is clearly thinking of non-Catholics; and since Eunomius distinctly opposed the tenet, and Augustine states that it was attributed by some to the Macedonians or Semiarians, we may fairly assume that it was practically confined to that party[2]. But that it had a very limited acceptance even amongst Semiarians seems clear from the silence of contemporary writers on the Doctrine of the Holy Spirit. If "most "Christians about the middle of the fourth century" had still to learn that the Holy Spirit is personal, how came it to pass that the Catholic theology of the time was content to establish His Deity? Such a book as St Basil's treatise on the Holy Spirit passes over the question of His personal existence altogether; the writer proceeds at once to his task of shewing that the

---

[1] *or. theol.* v (=xxxi) τὸ πνεῦμα τὸ ἅγιον Σαδδουκαῖοι μὲν οὐδὲ εἶναι τὸ παράπαν ἐνόμισαν...Ἑλλήνων δὲ οἱ θεολογικώτεροι...ἐφαντάσθησαν...νοῦν τοῦ παντός...προσαγορεύσαντες. τῶν δὲ καθ᾽ ἡμᾶς σοφῶν οἱ μὲν ἐνέργειαν τοῦτο ὑπέλαβον, οἱ δὲ κτίσμα, οἱ δὲ θεόν, οἱ δὲ οὐκ ἔγνωσαν ὁπότερον τούτων.

[2] *de haer. lib.* § 52 quamuis a non-nullis perhibeantur non deum sed deitatem patris et filii dicere Spiritum Sanctum, et nullam propriam habere substantiam. The view was however capable of an orthodox presentation; cf. *de fide et symb.* 19, 20, *de Trin.* xv. 27.

personal Holy Ghost is Divine. What were the influences, or where is the writing, to which the Church
owed her conversion to the doctrine of the personality
of the Holy Ghost? " The scientific Greek theology
"of the day" is responsible for having moulded earlier
conceptions into a consistent dogma, and provided them
with a nicely balanced terminology; but it is certainly
innocent of the creation of an idea which is as old as the
·Fourth Gospel and the Epistles of St Paul, and which
we have seen reflected continuously, although with
varying distinctness, in Church teaching from the end
of the first century.

But Professor Harnack proceeds: " Whoever, there-
" fore, introduces the doctrine of the Three Persons of
" the Godhead into the Creed, explains it contrary to
" its original meaning, and alters its true sense. Such
" an alteration was, of course, demanded of all Chris-
" tians from the end of the fourth century onwards, if
" they did not wish to expose themselves to the charge
" of heresy and its penalties."

It is remarkable that this vital alteration in the Faith
was not followed by an alteration in the Western Creed.
That Creed was in a fluid state until the eighth century,
yet no Western Church shewed the faintest desire to
modify the articles which relate to the Son and the
Holy Ghost. It would have been easy and even natural
to transfer to the Western Creed the definitions of the
Creed which was believed to have been accepted at
Constantinople; and it may with some confidence be
assumed that this would have been done if there had
been the least consciousness on the part of the Western

Church that she had executed the change of front imputed to her.

But there was no such consciousness either in East or West. The adherents of the Nicene theology protested from the first that they had changed nothing. The party represented at Nicaea by Eusebius of Caesarea have been called "the conservatives," and the name may be justified by their dislike of new phraseology[1]; but conservatism in regard to the essentials of theology was characteristic of the stoutest advocates of the Homoousion. Arianism, not the Nicene Faith, was the real offender; the serious innovations were on the side of those who denied the proper Deity of the Son and of the Spirit. If the Catholics used new terms, they did so in order to guard old beliefs; "malo enim "aliquid nouum commemorasse, quam impie respuisse[2]" is Hilary's sufficient answer to the charge of novelty. In the definitions subsequently introduced into the Creed of Jerusalem with the view of maintaining the Deity of the Holy Spirit, even verbal innovations seem to have been studiously avoided; the new matter was drawn almost exclusively from Scriptural sources; the word ὁμοούσιον was not applied to the Spirit, nor was He even called God. It may be said that this anxiety to keep within the limits of a Scriptural vocabulary was the fruit of policy; but the careful student of the Catholic writers of this epoch will recognise in it a deeper purpose. From Athanasius to Gregory of Nazianzus there comes an unbroken appeal to Holy Scripture and Catholic tradition, which repels the unworthy suspicion that the great Nicene teachers were guilty of consciously tampering with the ancient faith.

[1] See however Bright, *Waymarks*, p. 368 f.    [2] *de synod.* 82.

Did they, then, unconsciously and against their will change the current of Christian thought, and create the doctrine of a hypostatic Trinity? Harnack elsewhere attributes the change more especially to the Cappadocians[1]. It was the work of the second half of the fourth century. Let us, then, refer to earlier writers who cannot be suspected of Cappadocian orthodoxy. (1) The Creed of the martyr Lucian confesses that "the names of Father, Son, and Holy Ghost are not "mere otiose titles, but accurately represent the hypo- "stasis, order, and glory proper to Those Who bear "them, so that they are Three in hypostasis, although "One in their perfect harmony (τῇ μὲν ὑποστάσει τρία, "τῇ δὲ συμφωνίᾳ ἕν)[2]." (2) Eusebius of Caesarea, following the suggestion of Origen, speaks of the Holy Spirit as "the Third Power, above every created nature "—first of all the intelligent essences which have their "being through the Son, but third in order from the "First Cause[3]." (3) Cyril of Jerusalem, writing before the middle year of the century, teaches catechumens and the newly baptized: "Our hope is in the Father, "the Son, and the Holy Ghost; we preach not three "gods, but One God through One Son together with the "Holy Spirit—we neither divide the Holy Trinity, as "the manner of some is, nor work confusion, as the "Sabellians do." Of the Holy Ghost, Cyril remarks that He "is equal in dignity with the Father and the "Son"; "the Spirit is a living principle and possesses "a substantial existence (ζῶν καὶ ὑφεστός), and is ever "present with the Father and the Son[4]."

---

[1] e.g. *Dogmengeschichte* ed. 3, II. p. 283.
[2] Hahn, p. 185 f.
[3] *de eccl. theol.* iii. 6.
[4] *cat.* iv. 16, xvii. 5.

These statements vary in precision and in nearness of approach to the theology of the Cappadocian fathers; but they agree with one another and with the later teaching of the century in their practical recognition of a hypostatic Trinity. Yet the first two at least are less explicit than passages which might be quoted from writers of the third century, and the third is in harmony with the best teaching of the second. It is not pretended that the dogmatic language of individual teachers in the second century is always consistent with the riper convictions of the post-Nicene age. Like all pioneers, Justin, Tertullian, Origen, occasionally started on a false track; yet on the whole they moved upon lines which eventually led to the decisions of Nicaea and Constantinople. Of an essentially unequal Trinity, of a Son of God whose filial relations began with His human life, of an impersonal Spirit of God not to be distinguished from the 'energy' of the Father and the Son, they betray no knowledge. These were actual creations of the third century or of the fourth, and the Church disowned them as soon as their nature was clearly seen. The work of the great Nicene theologians was not primarily constructive; their first business was to refute novel and strange teaching. But the refutation of heresy has always served as an opportunity for a fresh illumination of the truth, and it was thus in the fourth century. The primitive faith in Father, Son, and Holy Ghost, grew under the hands of the great Greek theologians into a dogma, i.e., it acquired philosophical expression and a fixed terminology. But it ought to be possible to distinguish between the formulation of a doctrine and its creation. According to Professor Harnack the theology of the later Church was created by the genius of a handful of Catholic preachers and writers who lived in the second half of the fourth century. It has been the purpose of these chapters to shew that, while Catholic theology is indebted to these Fathers for much of its philosophical form and literary dress, its substance is due to the teaching of our Lord and of the Apostolic age, jealously preserved and gradually assimilated by successive generations of the Ante-Nicene Church.

## IV.

IN the Roman Creed of the fourth century the Miraculous Conception occupied, as it now occupies in the Apostles' Creed, the foremost place among the facts of the life of Christ. *Qui natus est*—so ran the Creeds both of Aquileia and of Rome—*de Spiritu Sancto ex Maria uirgine.* The words were slightly varied in some recensions ; Marcellus read, "Who was born of the "Holy Ghost *and* the Virgin Mary," and the same variation is exhibited in the Creeds of Codex Laudianus and the Athelstan Psalter[1]. The later paraphrase, *Qui conceptus est de Spiritu Sancto, natus ex Maria uirgine,* appears first in a series of sermons ascribed to Augustine[2], and in Gallican formularies[3], whence it passed into our present Creed. But it adds nothing of importance to the teaching of the fourth century form, and the only question which concerns us now is whether the substance of the article may be safely attributed to the earliest Creed of the Roman Church. Of this there seems to be little doubt. Both Irenaeus and Tertullian

---

[1] ἐκ πνεύματος ἀγίου καὶ Μαρίας τῆς παρθένου (Marcell., Ath.) ; de Spiritu sancto et Maria uirgine (*cod. Laud.*). So also MS. Reg. 2 A xx. and the Creeds in Aug. *Serm.* 212 —214, Nicetas, Facundus Herm., Hildefonsus Tolet. (Hahn, pp. 22,

26, 34, 36).

[2] *App. serm.* 240—244.

[3] e.g. in the *traditio symboli* of the *Missale Gallicanum uetus* (Muratori, ii. 710), "qui conceptus est de Spiritu Sancto, natus est de Maria uirgine."

give the Virgin-Birth a place in the Rule of Faith, and
Tertullian in one of his expositions of the Faith con-
nects with it a descent of the Holy Spirit[1]. No fact of
the Evangelical history was more firmly or generally
believed by the generation which gave shape to the
Western Creed. This is fully admitted by Dr Harnack,
who writes : " By the middle or probably soon after the
" beginning of the second century this belief had become
"an established part of the Church tradition." Nevertheless he contends that the belief was subapostolic
only, not Apostolic; "it is one of the best established
"results of history that the clause does not belong to
"the earliest Gospel preaching."

In examining this statement we will begin with the
middle of the second century, about which there is no
doubt, and work our way back with the view of dis-
covering when and how this belief took its rise. Justin's
writings will be the natural starting-point. From Justin's
point of view the Miraculous Conception is inseparable
from the Incarnation. The point of interest with him is
the virginity of Mary[2], and not the office ascribed to the
Holy Spirit; when he refers to the latter, he gives us
to understand that he identifies the ἅγιον πνεῦμα of
the Conception with the Logos and not with the Third
Person of the Trinity[3]. But it is a definite article in his
creed that the Logos was born without the intervention
of a human father. The miracle was foretold by the

---

[1] Iren. i. 10. 1 καὶ τὴν ἐκ παρθένου
γέννησιν. Tert. *de uel. uirg.* 1 natum ex Maria uirgine; *adu. Prax.* 2
missum a Patre in uirginem et ex
ea natum ; *de praescr.* 13 delatum
ex Spiritu Patris Dei et uirtute in
uirginem Mariam, carnem factum in
utero eius et ex ea natum.

[2] *apol.* i. 21 ἄνευ ἐπιμιξίας. 22 διὰ
παρθένου. Cf. *ib.* 32, 33, 63.
[3] *ib.* 31, 33; in the latter chapter
Justin says plainly, Τὸ πνεῦμα οὖν
καὶ τὴν δύναμιν τὴν παρὰ τοῦ θεοῦ
οὐδὲν ἄλλο νοῆσαι θέμις ἢ τὸν λόγον,
ὃς καὶ πρωτότοκος τῷ θεῷ ἐστιν.

Hebrew prophets, and certain stories in the Greek mythology were malicious attempts on the part of the demons to caricature the event by anticipation[1]. These statements appear in the first *Apology*, and they shew that the belief was at this time disclosed to the heathen without reserve. With Trypho the Jew Justin is equally free; the *Dialogue* is full of the subject, which is treated as one of the commonplaces of Christianity; and we get an insight into the reasons which led Christians of that age to attach so much importance to it. The Virgin's Son is, as such, "without sin" (δίχα ἁμαρτίας, c. 23); He is true man, but not ἄνθρωπος ἐξ ἀνθρώπου (c. 48). By her obedience to the call of God the Virgin reversed the disobedience of Eve[2]. Two important facts in the history of the belief are incidentally mentioned. (1) The Jews were so familiar with the Christian doctrine in this matter that they had begun to meet the argument based on Isa. vii. 14 by denying that עַלְמָה is rightly represented by παρθένος and substituting νεᾶνις for the rendering of the LXX.[3] (2) The Virgin-Birth was consistently rejected by those Christians—a minority, as Justin implies—who held the adoptianist or elective view of our Lord's Sonship[4].

Going backwards, we find the belief in the Virgin-

---

[1] *apol.* 54 ὅτε δὲ ἤκουσαν [οἱ δαίμονες] διὰ τοῦ ἄλλου προφήτου Ἡσαίου λεχθὲν ὅτι διὰ παρθένου τεχθήσεται... τὸν Περσέα λεχθῆναι προεβάλλοντο.

[2] *dial.* 100 ἵνα καὶ δι' ἧς ὁδοῦ ἡ ἀπὸ τοῦ ὄφεως παρακοὴ τὴν ἀρχὴν ἔλαβε, διὰ ταύτης τῆς ὁδοῦ καὶ κατάλυσιν λάβῃ· παρθένος γὰρ οὖσα Εὔα καὶ ἄφθορος, τὸν λόγον τὸν ἀπὸ τοῦ ὄφεως συλλαβοῦσα, παρακοὴν καὶ θάνατον ἔτεκε· πίστιν δὲ καὶ χαρὰν λαβοῦσα Μαρία ἡ παρθένος, κ.τ.λ.

[3] *ib.* 43 ὑμεῖς καὶ οἱ διδάσκαλοι

ὑμῶν τολμᾶτε λέγειν μηδὲ εἰρῆσθαι ἐν τῇ προφητείᾳ τοῦ Ἡσαίου Ἰδοὺ ἡ παρθένος ἐν γαστρὶ ἕξει, ἀλλ' Ἰδοὺ ἡ νεᾶνις ἐν γ. λήψεται. Comp. Iren. *ap.* Euseb. *H. E.* v. 8, Orig. *c. Cels.* i. 34.

[4] *ib.* 48 καὶ γάρ εἰσί τινες, ὦ φίλοι, ἔλεγον, ἀπὸ τοῦ ἡμετέρου γένους ὁμολογοῦντες αὐτὸν Χριστὸν εἶναι, ἄνθρωπον δὲ ἐξ ἀνθρώπων γενόμενον ἀποφαινόμενοι· οἷς οὐ συντίθεμαι, οὐδ' ἂν πλεῖστοι ταὐτά μοι δοξάσαντες εἴποιεν.

Birth in Aristides, who seems to include it in his formal summary of Christian *credenda*. A comparison of the restored Greek apology with the Syriac and Armenian versions justifies us in attributing to Aristides himself the words ἐκ παρθένου γεννηθεὶς σάρκα ἀνέλαβε, and the preceding context in the Greek refers to the agency of the Holy Spirit[1].

The next step brings us to Ignatius. His witness is clear and emphatic. The classical passage is *Eph.* 19: "the prince of this world was ignorant of the virginity "of Mary and of her child-bearing." It was one of the mysteries which were 'wrought in the silence of God, 'but are now to be proclaimed to the world[2].' With regard to the fact Ignatius had no doubt; it was as certain in his eyes as the Crucifixion. Jesus Christ (he maintains against certain Docetic teachers) was truly born of a Virgin; truly nailed to the Cross for us in the flesh (*Trall.* 9, *Smyrn.* 1). It is important to observe that while Justin presses the Virgin-Birth against pagans and Jews, Ignatius asserts it against heresy. The heretics whom Ignatius wishes to refute appear not to have denied the fact, but they explained it away, as they explained away the Passion. The doctrine of the Miraculous Conception lent itself readily to the suggestion of unreality. Ignatius is not shaken

---

[1] Comp. J. R. Harris, *Aristides*, p. 24 f. Hennecke, p. 9. The full Greek text is ὁμολογεῖται ἐν πνεύματι ἁγίῳ ἀπ' οὐρανοῦ καταβὰς διὰ τὴν σωτηρίαν τῶν ἀνθρώπων, καὶ ἐκ παρθένου ἁγίας γεννηθεὶς ἀσπόρως τε καὶ ἀφθόρως σάρκα ἀνέλαβε. The words ἐν πνεύματι ἁγίῳ are not directly represented either in the Syriac or the Armenian: the former turns the sentence "It is said that God came down from heaven"; the latter paraphrases, "The Son...was manifested by the Holy Spirit"; but the Greek phrase has the true ring of the second century.

[2] *Eph.* 19 ἔλαθεν τὸν ἄρχοντα τοῦ αἰῶνος τούτου ἡ παρθενία Μαρίας καὶ ὁ τοκετὸς αὐτῆς, ὁμοίως καὶ ὁ θάνατος τοῦ κυρίου· τρία μυστήρια κραυγῆς, ἅτινα ἐν ἡσυχίᾳ θεοῦ ἐπράχθη.

by this circumstance; he asserts the reality of the event notwithstanding its supernatural character. It would have been comparatively easy to turn the Docetic position, if he could have replied that the Lord was born as other men are. But Ignatius knows nothing of such a doctrine, and the great Church over which he had presided and the Churches of Western Asia Minor to which he wrote were evidently involved in the same ignorance.

Before we attempt to get behind the age of Ignatius, it may be well to consider the attitude of second century heresy toward this belief. There were heretical Christians who rejected it altogether, as Justin tells us; and we have no difficulty in identifying them with the Ebionite school or its Gnostic exponents, the followers of Cerinthus and Carpocrates, and the early Ophites[1]. No critical grounds are stated for the repudiation of the doctrine by these heretics, whilst the exigencies of their dogmatic position supply an obvious motive. But the other and more important Gnostic schools, those whose tendency was Docetic rather than Ebionite, followed the Ignatian Docetae in accepting the Miraculous Conception, working it into their own systems in various shapes. So the Valentinians, both 'Italic' and 'Anatolic' (Hippol. vi. 35); so, too, Basilides (*ib.* vii. 26), and the later 'Docetae' described by Hippolytus (viii. 9), and the Gnostics of Irenaeus (iii. 11. 3). The fact was accepted by these heretics on the authority of the Gospels, and not as a tradition inherited from the Church; Hippolytus repre-

---

[1] Iren. i. 25. 1 Carpocrates autem et qui ab eo...Iesum...e Ioseph natum [esse dicunt]. *ib.* 26. 1 Cerinthus...Iesum subiecit [sc. Deo], non ex uirgine natum (impossibile enim hoc ei uisum est), fuisse autem eum Ioseph et Mariae filium similiter ut reliqui omnes homines. Comp. Hippol. vii. 32, 33. Similarly Justin the Ophite represented Jesus as the son of Joseph and Mary (Hippol. v. 26). Cf. *Asc. Isai.*, p. 54.

sents both the Valentinians and Basilides as appealing to St Luke.

A word may be said in passing as to the view which the Jews took of the Christian doctrine. They made no serious attempt to shew that our Lord was the Son of Joseph and Mary. Finding that the great majority of Christians, both Catholics and heretics, were agreed in denying the paternity of Joseph, they acquiesced in this belief, but used it as the occasion for a blasphemous libel, which was already familiar to Celsus in the eighth decade of the second century[1]. The true father of Jesus was, they said, a soldier named Pantheras. The story seems to have originated in a misunderstanding of the title Ben-Pandera[2], which was taken for a patronymic, but was probably an intentional misreading of Ben Parthena, the Virgin's Son. But why was the imaginary Pandera or Pantheras represented as a soldier? It has been suggested that the tale belongs to the time of Hadrian, when the Roman soldier was naturally execrated by the crushed and scattered race. If this conjecture be accepted as probable, the Jewish use of Pandera must be pushed back to a time anterior to Hadrian's war; and the impression is confirmed which has been received from the letters of Ignatius as to the wide diffusion of this belief among Christians of

---

[1] Orig. *c. Cels.* 28 προσωποποιεῖ Ἰουδαῖον αὐτῷ διαλεγόμενον τῷ Ἰησοῦ καὶ ἐλέγχοντα αὐτὸν περὶ πολλῶν μέν, ὡς οἴεται· πρῶτον δέ, ὡς πλασαμένου αὐτοῦ τὴν ἐκ παρθένου γένεσιν...φησὶ δὲ αὐτὴν [sc. τὴν Μαρίαν] καὶ ὑπὸ τοῦ γήμαντος...ἐξεῶσθαι, ἐλεγχθεῖσαν ὡς μεμοιχευμένην. § 32 ἀλλὰ γὰρ ἐπανέλθωμεν εἰς τὴν τοῦ Ἰουδαίου προσωποποιίαν ἐν ᾗ ἀναγέγραπται ἡ τοῦ Ἰησοῦ μήτηρ...τίκτουσα ἀπό τινος στρατιώτου Πανθήρα τοὔνομα.

[2] בן פנדרא is a common name of scorn for our Lord in the Talmud. On the whole subject see Laible, *Jesus Christus im Talmud*, pp. 9—26, or Streane, *J. C. in the Talmud*, p. 7 ff. Whatever the solution may be, there can be no doubt that Origen's criticism is just: ταῦτα πάντα ἀνέπλασαν ἐπὶ καθαιρέσει τῆς παραδόξου ἀπὸ ἁγίου πνεύματος συλλήψεως.

the generation which immediately followed the death
of St John.

What was the ultimate source of the belief? We
have seen that the Gnostic sects of the middle of the
century appealed to the Gospel of St Luke. Justin
similarly justifies his statements by the words "as we
"learned from the Memoirs" (*dial.* 105). His references
are for the most part to St Luke, but St Matthew
appears to be in view more than once (*dial.* 78, *apol.*
i. 33). Ignatius, on the other hand, seems to be independent of both narratives; if he leans to either, it is to
St Matthew, but on the whole his words leave the impression that he either refers to some third document
perhaps akin to our First Gospel, or is simply handing
on a fact which had been taught him orally, probably
when he first received the Faith. The latter supposition
carries us back, perhaps far back, into the first century[1].

We cannot, however, pursue this clue, and for further
light we must turn to the two Gospels which record the
Conception. Much has been made of the silence of
St Mark, but the argument *ex silentio* was never more
conspicuously misplaced; it is puerile to demand of a
record which professes to begin with the ministry of the
Baptist that it shall mention an event which preceded
the Baptist's birth. The plan of the Fourth Gospel
equally excludes a reference to the manner of our
Lord's entrance into the world; although the prominence given by St John to the Mother of the Lord
is favourable to the hypothesis that the Evangelist
was not ignorant of her peculiar privilege. In St
Luke, on the other hand, we might reasonably expect to find the fact recorded; had it been wanting

[1] See Lightfoot on Ign. *Eph.* 19.

our suspicions would have been awakened, for the author's purpose is to construct a biography, and he gathers from all the sources at his command. Hence the Nativity and the events which led up to it are an integral part of his story. Few will now contend that Marcion's mutilated Gospel, beginning as it did with an arbitrary fusion of Luke iii. 1, iv. 31, was the original St Luke. Yet if the first two chapters formed part of the original Gospel, our most important record of the Conception is carried back, let us say, to A.D. 75—80, a *terminus ad quem* for the publication of the third Gospel accepted by one of the most cautious and far-seeing of living New Testament scholars[1]. But we cannot stop there. The style of Luke i. 5—ii. 52 clearly points to sources older than the Gospel itself. There are indeed correspondences of style and vocabulary which connect this section with the rest of the Gospel, and shew that the whole book has passed through the hands of the same compiler[2]; yet the section betrays unmistakably, as we think, an independent origin. It has an archaic tone ; its thought and spirit are Judaeo-Christian ; the hymns which characterise it are permeated by the thought and language of the Old Testament ; the narrative preserves a simplicity which contrasts not only with St Luke's formal prologue, but with his rendering of the synoptic tradition. The whole section may thus with some confidence be traced to a source earlier than the Fall of Jerusalem, and probably supplied by the traditions

---

[1] Sanday, *Inspiration*, p. 277 ff. Harnack (*Chronologie*, pp. 250, 718) assigns it to the interval 78—93.

[2] See, *e.g.*, Sanday, *Gospels in the Second Century*, p. 222 ff.

of the Church of Jerusalem.   And bearing in mind
St Luke's plan of pushing his enquiries back as far as
he could go, it is scarcely too bold to suppose that he
believed himself to be in possession of a narrative which
came from the Mother of the Lord.   The Church over
which James the Lord's brother presided and of which
Mary herself had been a member during her residence
at Jerusalem with the Apostle John, would have been
the natural repository of such a reminiscence.   There,
if anywhere, the hymns of Zacharias, Mary, and Simeon,
would have been treasured—perhaps liturgically used
and moulded into their present form.

The narrative of the Conception in the first Gospel
is absolutely independent of the narrative in the third.
They are not simply distinct accounts proceeding from
two independent observers, but they cover almost
entirely different ground.   Jóseph is the centre of St
Matthew's story, as Mary of St Luke's.   The latter
story deals with the Annunciation and Visitation, the
former with a revelation to Joseph made subsequently
to the Annunciation, and probably after Mary's return
from Judaea.   The work of the harmonist is here simple
and straightforward ; Luke i. 26—56 is naturally followed by Matt. i. 18—25, and Luke ii. 1—38 by Matt.
ii. 1.   Yet this ready locking together of the parts of
the story cannot be due to a desire on the part of either
Evangelist to supplement the work of the other.   St
Matthew seems to write in entire ignorance of the
circumstance that the scene of the events which preceded the Nativity was laid in Galilee.   St Luke allows
no interval for the flight into Egypt.   Tatian, who
arranged the two accounts nearly in the manner suggested above, was evidently perplexed when he reached

Luke ii. 39[1], and endeavoured to meet the difficulty by placing Matt. ii. 1 after the return into Galilee and substituting a vague phrase for St Matthew's note of time. It would have been better to recognise that St Luke was ignorant of the visit of the Magi and the flight. Ignorance of this kind does not affect the credibility of a writer with regard to matters which he professes to know, but it demonstrates his independence.

It is natural to conjecture that St Matthew's story originated with Joseph, as St Luke's with the Mother of the Lord[2]. Of Joseph we have no certain information later than our Lord's twelfth year, but the committal of the Mother to St John is usually regarded as evidence that he died before the Crucifixion. Probably his death preceded the Baptism, for throughout the Ministry the Mother appears in company with the Lord's brethren. But if Joseph died in Galilee before the Ministry, his account of the events which preceded the Nativity might have been long in gaining circulation. It might have escaped even the vigilance of St Luke, and have formed one of the latest accretions to the narrative of the Gospels.

Such a hypothesis may be thought to account for certain appearances in the text of Matt. i. 16 ff. Epiphanius relates that the first Gospel was used in a shorter form by the Ebionites, Cerinthians, and Carpocratians. The Ebionites omitted the first two chapters, the Cerinthians retained the genealogy, for " they wished to shew "from the genealogy that our Lord was the son of "Joseph and Mary[3]." It is precarious to place faith in

---

[1] Ciasca, p. 5: cf. Dr Hamlyn Hill's *Earliest Life of Christ*, p. 50, *n.*

[2] This view is well stated by Canon Gore, *Incarnation*, p. 78;

on the whole question see his *Dissertations*, pp. 3—68, 292 ff.

[3] *haer.* xxxviii. 5 χρῶνται γὰρ τῷ κατὰ Ματθαῖον εὐαγγελίῳ ἀπὸ μέρους

Epiphanius's statements, especially when they concern the wrong-doings of heretics; but if we may trust him here, the Cerinthian Gospel must have differed from our own by the absence not only of c. i. 18—25, but of a part of c. i. 16. Now it is remarkable that this verse exists in a variety of forms which suggests some early disturbance of the text. Most of our Greek MSS. read: Ἰακὼβ δὲ ἐγέννησεν τὸν Ἰωσὴφ τὸν ἄνδρα Μαρίας, ἐξ ἧς ἐγεννήθη Ἰησοῦς ὁ λεγόμενος Χριστός. But two cursives (346, of the Ferrar group, and 556 = 543 Greg.) substitute for τὸν ἄνδρα, κ.τ.λ., the words ᾧ μνηστευθεῖσα παρθένος Μαριὰμ ἐγέννησεν Ἰησοῦν τὸν λεγόμενον Χριστόν, and this alternative ending to the verse is supported in substance by seven MSS. of the pre-Hieronymian Latin[1], and by the Curetonian Syriac. A second and more serious variant occurs in the newly-discovered Sinaitic Syriac, which presupposes the Greek Ἰωσήφ, ᾧ ἐμνηστεύθη παρθένος Μαριάμ, ἐγέννησεν Ἰησοῦν τὸν λεγόμενον Χριστόν. These facts involve the ending of verse 16 in some uncertainty, and lend plausibility to the idea that the verse did not originally contain the words which assert the virginity of the Lord's mother. But the evidence is at present far

καὶ οὐχ ὅλῳ, ἀλλὰ διὰ τὴν γενεαλογίαν τὴν ἔνσαρκον. *ib.* xxx. 14 ὁ μὲν γὰρ Κήρινθος καὶ Καρποκρᾶς τῷ αὐτῷ χρώμενοι δῆθεν παρ' αὐτοῖς εὐαγγελίῳ ἀπὸ τῆς ἀρχῆς τοῦ κατὰ Ματθαῖον εὐαγγελίου διὰ τῆς γενεαλογίας βούλονται παριστᾶν ἐκ σπέρματος Ἰωσὴφ καὶ Μαρίας εἶναι τὸν Χριστόν· οὗτοι δὲ [οἱ Ἐβιωναῖοι] ἄλλα τινὰ διανοοῦνται· παρακόψαντες γὰρ τὰς παρὰ τῷ Ματθαίῳ γενεαλογίας ἄρχονται τὴν ἀρχὴν ποιεῖσθαι, ὡς προεῖπον, λέγοντες ὅτι Ἐγένετο κ.τ.λ. (Mt. iii. 1). Comp. Westcott, *Canon*, p. 277, *n.* 2.

[1] Cod. k reads *cui desponsata uirgo* M. *genuit Iesum Christum*; d gives *cui desp. u. M. peperit C. I.*; b, *cui desp. erat u. M., u. autem M. genuit I. C.*; c, *cui desp. u. M., M. autem genuit I. qui dicitur Christus*; ag[1] have *cui desp. u. M. genuit I. qui uocatur* (a, *dicitur*) *Christus*; q has *cui desp. M. genuit I. qui uoc. Chr.* Syr.ᶜᵘ· renders "to whom was betrothed Mary the Virgin who bore J. C."; Arm., "[to whom having been betrothed M. the Virgin], from whom was born J. who was named C."

from sufficient to justify this conclusion[1]; and if it were stronger, the phenomena might be explained with almost equal probability on the hypothesis of early mutilation. In the mean while the matter may be regarded with comparative equanimity by those who believe in the miracle of the Virgin-Birth. Even if it should appear that in the original Matthew the genealogy ended with the formula "Joseph begat Jesus," the words would no more be a denial of the miracle than St Luke's references to Joseph as "the father" (Luke ii. 33) and to Joseph and Mary as "the parents" of the Lord (ib. 27, 41). If St Matthew's account of the Angel's message to Joseph could be shewn to have been inserted in the Gospel after its publication, the circumstance would prove nothing more than that the facts were unknown to the writer of the original draft ; nor would it materially weaken their claim to be regarded as historical.

We have then, in any case, two absolutely independent narratives of events connected with the Miraculous Conception, one an integral part of the third Gospel, the other a part of the first Gospel in all existing MSS. and versions. Apart from the question of the date of the completion of our present Matthew, both these documents shew every indication of being genuine products of the first century, probably of a generation anterior to the Fall of Jerusalem. St Luke's story has the true ring of the primitive age ; St Matthew's is shewn by its independence of St Luke's to be earlier than the publication of the latter. There is probability in the conjecture which traces them respectively to the Mother of the Lord and His supposed father.

---

[1] See Bp Westcott's remarks in WH[2], *Notes on Select Readings*, p. 141.

Nevertheless, Dr Harnack contends, the Conception "does not belong to the earliest Gospel preaching." This may at once be conceded, if the words are restricted to their narrowest sense. The earliest Gospel preaching was limited to the witness borne by the Twelve to the things which they had seen and heard. It began, therefore, with the baptism of John, reaching from the commencement of the Lord's Galilean Ministry to His Ascension, but finding its culminating point in the Resurrection (Acts i. 21, 22). The second Gospel, in its completed form, may be taken to correspond as nearly as possible with this original cycle of teaching ; and the Gospel of St Mark, as we are often reminded, knows nothing of the miracles which attended the Lord's Conception and Nativity. It is urged, however, that the doctrine of the Conception is equally absent from St Paul's teaching. As a matter of fact we have little direct evidence to shew what St Paul's presentment of the Gospel history may have been, unless we suppose it to be mirrored in the Gospel of St Luke, which gives us our fullest account of the event. But not to press this point, it is obviously unsafe to argue from St Paul's silence, since he is equally silent on many other matters which certainly formed part of the Apostolic teaching. The purpose of his Epistles is to teach the religion and the ethics of the Faith, not to restate its historical basis ; the latter was the work of the catechist, rather than of an Apostle who had received a special mission of another kind. It would have been a departure from St Paul's plan, if he had directly referred to the fact of the Conception. But there are portions of his teaching where the event may well have been in the background of his thought, as when he speaks of our Lord as 'the 'heavenly man,' insists on His absolute sinlessness, and describes Him as 'made of a woman,' in a context where it would have been at least as natural to represent Him as the son of Joseph had He believed Him to be such[1]. On the other hand no adverse conclusion can fairly be drawn from Rom. i. 3, 'made of the seed of David 'according to the flesh,' as if the words asserted the paternity of Joseph. Ignatius more than once combines in the same sentence the Davidic descent with the Virgin-Birth[2].

But the right of the Church in the second century to teach the doctrine does not turn upon the question whether it was taught by the Apostles or in their life-time. If an important fact connected with the Incarnation did not come to light until St Paul had passed away, it was none the less worthy of a place in the historical portion of the Creed so soon as it became part of the common heritage of the Christian Society. The appearance in the first and third Gospels of two inde-pendent accounts, gathered from the stores of the primi-tive Palestinian Church, would have been justification enough. But as far as we can judge, the belief was older than the publication of the Gospels. When it first appears in the letters of Ignatius, it was already accepted without question from Antioch to Ephesus. Yet some of the Churches by which it was confessed had received the faith from St Paul, and all were fresh from the teaching of St John.

[1] See an article by C. J. H. Ropes, "Born of the Virgin Mary," in the *Andover Review*, Nov.—Dec. 1893, pp. 704—707; and cf. Knowling, *Witness of the Epistles*, p. 274 ff.
[2] *Eph.* 18, *Trall.* 9, *Smyrn.* 1.

## V.

"THE words *He descended into Hell* are not in the
"Creed of the Church of Rome." So Rufinus tells us at
the end of the fourth century. He adds that they were
unknown to the Churches of the East[1]. This is true so
far as regards the baptismal creeds; no Eastern form
contains the clause or anything corresponding to it.
Yet, before Rufinus wrote his commentary, the doctrine
of the Descent had found a place in three synodical
declarations, put forth by the Arian assemblies gathered
at Sirmium, Nicé, and Constantinople, in the years 359
and 360[2]. The wording of these manifestos will repay
examination and comparison.

| SIRMIUM. | NICÉ. | CONSTANTINOPLE. |
|---|---|---|
| Καὶ εἰς τὰ καταχθόνια κατελθόντα, καὶ τὰ ἐκεῖσε οἰκονομήσαντα· ὃν πυλωροὶ ᾄδου ἰδόντες ἔφριξαν. | Καὶ ταφέντα καὶ εἰς τὰ καταχθόνια κατελθόντα· ὃν αὐτὸς ὁ ᾄδης ἐτρόμασε. | Καὶ ταφέντα καὶ εἰς τὰ καταχθόνια κατεληλυθότα· ὅντινα καὶ αὐτὸς ὁ ᾄδης ἔπτηξεν. |

It will be observed that the earliest of the three
forms omits καὶ ταφέντα, as if it were implied in the new
phrase which follows[3]; the second and third replace καὶ

---

[1] *in symb.* 18 sciendum sane est
quod in ecclesiae Romanae symbolo
non habetur additum *descendit ad
inferna*, sed neque in Orientis eccle-
siis habetur hic sermo.

[2] Hahn, pp. 125—9.
[3] Comp. Rufinus, *l.c.* uis tamen
uerbi eadem uidetur esse in eo quod
*sepultus* uidetur (cf. *infr.* § 28).

ταφέντα, but retain the new words. All the three are remarkable for the dramatic tone in which they describe the Descent. The Sirmian phrase rests ultimately on Job xxxviii. 17 (LXX. πυλωροὶ δὲ ᾅδου ἰδόντες σε ἔπτηξαν); but the reference is probably at second hand, for the passage in Job had been applied to our Lord by Athanasius[1] and Cyril of Jerusalem[2]. Cyril, whose influence is seen in other features of the Sirmian ecthesis, assigns great importance to the Descent, admitting it into his exposition of the ten "necessary dogmas[3]." With regard to the personification of Hades which appears in the two later forms, this new feature may have been borrowed directly from St Paul (1 Cor. xv. 55, after Hosea xiii. 14) or from St John (Apoc. vi. 8, xx. 13, 14).

The rhetorical language in which these Councils describe the Descent seems to be characteristic of the fourth century : but the belief existed from the first, and at a very early period gathered round itself a number of remarkable accretions. Our Lord, it was said, had descended in order to visit and instruct the patriarchs and prophets of the Old Testament, or to raise them to a higher state of existence, or in some cases to restore them to life on earth. A similar *descensus ad inferos* was attributed by some early writers to the Forerunner, and to the Apostles and the first generation of believers. How wide a range these ideas attained will be seen when we add that in one form or another they occur in Ignatius, Hermas,

---

[1] *fragm. in Luc.* x. 22; *or. c. Arian.* iii. 57.

[2] *catech.* xi. 23, xiv. 19: ἐξεπλάγη ὁ θάνατος θεωρήσας καινόν τινα κατελθόντα εἰς ᾅδην...τίνος ἕνεκεν, ὦ πυλωροὶ ᾅδου, τοῦτον ἰδόντες ἐπτήξασθε;

Comp. Heurtley, pp. 136—7.

[3] Cp. Gwatkin, *Studies*, pp. 132—3. Cyril's *catecheses* were delivered a full decade before the 'dated creed.'

Justin, Irenaeus, the Petrine Gospel, Clement of Alex-
andria, Hippolytus, Origen[1], the Edessan document cited
by Eusebius (*H. E.* i. 13), and the Teaching of Addai[2].

Can we trace these aspects of the Descent to the
Apostolic age? It is natural to think of 1 Pet. iv. 6 (καὶ
νεκροῖς εὐηγγελίσθη); but 1 Pet. iii. 18, 19 seems to limit
this preaching to the generation who perished in the
Flood. Nor is there any considerable evidence that either
of these passages influenced the thought of the second
century. There is a possible reference to them in the
Petrine Gospel (ἐκήρυξας τοῖς κοιμωμένοις)[3], and they
may also be contemplated in the saying of the Elder
(possibly Pothinus, Irenaeus's predecessor in the see of
Lyons[4]) quoted by Irenaeus (iv. 27. 2). But no direct
appeal is made to St Peter in any of the numerous
references to the Descent; the earliest quotation of
1 Pet. iv. 6 we have been able to find is in Cyprian's
*Testimonia*[5]. On the whole it is scarcely possible
to account for the early legends of the Descent by
supposing them to be based upon reminiscences of St
Peter's words. Their general acceptance may with more
probability be traced to the influence of some early
teaching which strove to combine the scattered hints of
Scripture, as that (e.g.) of the *apocryphon* which is boldly
said by Justin (*dial.* 70) to have been removed by the
Jews from their copies of Jeremiah, and which Irenaeus
ascribes once (iv. 22. 1) to Jeremiah and once (iii. 20. 4)

[1] See Lightfoot's note on Ign. *Magn.* 9.

[2] Cureton, *Ancient Syriac documents*, p. 7.

[3] *Akhmîm fragment*, p. 19, *n.*

[4] Lightfoot, *Essays on Supernatural Religion*, p. 266. The words of the Elder are: Dominum in ea quae sunt sub terra descendisse euangelizantem et illis aduentum suum, remissione peccatorum existente his qui credunt in eum.

[5] ii. 27 item illic: In hoc enim et mortuis praedicatum est ut suscitentur. *Ut suscitentur* seems to interpret ἵνα...ζῶσιν as = ἵνα ἐγερθῶσιν.

to Isaiah, and which in three other places (iv. 33. 1, 12 ;
v. 31. 1) he quotes anonymously. The words are: "The
"Lord God, the Holy One of Israel, remembered His
"dead, which slept in the dust of the earth, and de-
"scended to them, to preach unto them His salvation[1]."
One of the sources of this saying is betrayed by the
words εἰς γῆν χώματος, an inversion of the phrase in
Dan. xii. 2 (Th.)[2]; and the author had also in view,
besides the passage in 1 Peter, the incident recorded in
Matt. xxvii. 52, for he has altered Theodotion's καθευδόντων into St Matthew's κεκοιμημένων[3]. His words,
possibly a fragment of a primitive homily, commended
themselves so fully to the subapostolic age that before
Justin's time they had acquired a place in some Christian
copies of the Prophets.

A remarkable contrast is presented when we turn
from the rhetorical descriptions of the fourth century
and the simpler yet fanciful conceptions of the second,
to the article in the Apostles' Creed which announces
the fact of the Descent. Here both words and teaching
are directly Scriptural: *Descendit in infernum* (*ad infernum, ad inferna*) are Old Latin and Vulgate renderings
of יָרַד שְׁאֹלָה, LXX. εἰς ᾅδου κατέβη. The clause carries
Rufinus back to his Psalter, and he quotes Ps. xv (xvi). 10,
xxi (xxii). 16, xxix (xxx). 4, 10, lxviii (lxix). 3[4]; for the
phrase he might have referred to Ps. liv (lv). 16, cxiii. 25
(cxv. 17), cxxxviii (cxxxix). 8. Of these passages the

---

[1] ἐμνήσθη δὲ Κύριος ὁ θεὸς ἅγιος
(ἀπό, Just.; *sanctus*, Iren.; cf. the
vv. ll. in 3 Macc. vi. 9) Ἰσραὴλ τῶν
νεκρῶν αὐτοῦ τῶν κεκοιμημένων εἰς
γῆν χώματος, καὶ κατέβη πρὸς αὐτοὺς
εὐαγγελίσασθαι αὐτοῖς τὸ σωτήριον
αὐτοῦ. Cf. 4 Esdr. ii. 31.

[2] πολλοὶ τῶν καθευδόντων ἐν γῆς
χώματι ἐξεγερθήσονται. The *apocryphon* follows the original אַדְמַת
עָפָר. Comp. Bevan, *Daniel*, p. 201.

[3] The same variant occurs in
*Const. Ap.* v. 7.

[4] *in symb.* § 28.

first had been cited by St Peter on the Day of Pentecost,
and applied to our Lord's departure from the body in a
manner which alone might have been sufficient to justify
the use of the words in the Creed.　If we ask ourselves
what meaning was attached to such words by the primitive Church of Jerusalem, it is natural to seek an
answer in the interpretation of the corresponding Hebrew
phrase.　"Sheol," writes Professor Schultz, "is not the
"grave itself, for even when there is no grave, Sheol is
"thought of as the abode of the departed.　It is the
"dwelling-place of the dead, who rest there after the joy
"and the suffering of life[1]."　Since the body was com-
mitted to the depths of the earth, it was natural to asso-
ciate the condition of the dead with the thought of an
underworld, and to speak of a 'descent' into Sheol.
The primitive Church took over these ideas, and the
language in which they were clothed ; that our Lord at
His death descended into Hades not only accorded with
the Psalmist's prophecy, but was involved in her belief
of the reality of His human nature.　St Paul followed
upon the same lines, boldly adapting Deut. xxx. 13 to
the fact of the Descent (Rom. x. 7)[2].　The Descent into
Hades was in the Pauline Christology the lowest point
in the κατάβασις which preceded the ἀνάβασις of the
Incarnate Son (Eph. iv. 9)[3].　Obedience even unto death
secured for Him the sovereignty of the underworld (τὰ
καταχθόνια) ; His descent thither was the pledge of His
lordship over it (Phil. ii. 10)[4].

---

[1] *O. T. Theology* (E. T.), ii. p. 323.

[2] For Τίς διαπεράσει ἡμῖν εἰς τὸ πέραν τῆς θαλάσσης; (Deut. *l. c.* LXX.) the Apostle substitutes, Τίς καταβήσεται εἰς τὴν ἄβυσσον; commenting τοῦτ' ἔστιν, Χριστὸν ἐκ νεκρῶν ἀναγαγεῖν. The ambiguous

ἄβυσσον covers both θάλασσαν and ᾅδην (cf. Ps. cvi (cvii). 26, Luke viii. 31).

[3] τὸ δὲ ἀνέβη, τί ἐστιν εἰ μὴ ὅτι καὶ κατέβη εἰς τὰ κατώτερα μέρη τῆς γῆς;

[4] ἵνα πᾶν γόνυ κάμψῃ...καταχθο-

At what precise time these primitive ideas took their place under a severely simple form in the baptismal Creed, we cannot say. We meet with the clause for the first time in the Aquileian Creed of the fourth century, but it can hardly have been then of recent introduction. The Church of Aquileia laid claim to an antiquity scarcely inferior to that of the Roman Church. St Mark was regarded as its founder[1], and the martyrologies speak of an Aquileian Bishop who suffered under Nero. No reliance, of course, can be placed upon these stories of a later age, yet they witness to a belief which on the whole was probably sound. The importance of Aquileia, which afterwards secured to its Bishop metropolitan rank and an independence shared in Italy only by the see of Milan, points to an early establishment of the Church in that city. The Aquileian Church received her Creed from Rome, but exercised the right of modifying the original form. To the first article she added the words "invisible and impassible," as a protest, Rufinus tells us, against Sabellianism; whilst against a false spiritualising she maintained "the resurrection of *this* "flesh." It is at least probable that the words *descendit ad inferna* were introduced with a like purpose, to meet some heresy; and the Docetic tendency of the latter part of the second century[2] suggests itself as likely to have supplied the occasion. Rufinus in any case has lost the clue, and this circumstance alone would lead us to suppose that the addition was made long before his time. Moreover the simplicity of the words points us to the early days of the Aquileian Church. We shall

---

υἱῶν (*infernorum*), καὶ πᾶσα γλῶσσα ἐξομολογήσηται ὅτι κύριος Ἰησοῦς Χριστός.

[1] See the writer's *Gospel acc. to* *St Mark*, p. xxiii.

[2] Comp. e.g. the sequel to the Lord's Death imagined by Pseudo-Peter, *ev.* 9.

perhaps not be far wrong if we assign the clause to the end of the second century, or the beginning of the third.

From Aquileia the reference to the Descent made its way further west. It occurs in the Creed of Venantius Fortunatus, who was Bishop of Poitiers in the last years of the sixth century, but in early life had resided at Aquileia. Here it appears to take the place of *et sepultus*, as in the Sirmian manifesto of 359[1]; but in the Gallican and Spanish creeds of the next half century the two clauses stand side by side, and from that time in Creeds of the Gallican recension they kept the position which they still occupy.

The history is an instructive one. An article of the faith, which is neither Roman nor Eastern, has established itself in the Creed of Western Christendom through the influence of a remote Church represented by a Gallican prelate who had spent his early days in North-East Italy. It did not reach Gaul, as far as we can judge, till the end of the sixth century. But it came from one of the earliest forms of the baptismal Creed; it reflected an absolutely primitive belief: it is expressed in the phraseology of the early Latin Bible. Why should this clause be regarded with misgiving because of the accident of its Aquileian origin? Professor Harnack insists that "the clause is too weak to maintain its "ground beside the others, as equally independent and "authoritative." In what its weakness lies, the Professor fails to point out; to us it appears to possess in a very high degree the strength which comes from primitive simplicity and a wise reserve. Each of the great Churches

---

[1] Hahn, p. 46: crucifixus sub Pontio Pilato, descendit ad infernum. Comp. pp. 66, 76, 77 f.

in ancient Christendom had its special contribution to bring to the fulness of Christian faith and life. It was the privilege of the Church of Aquileia to hand down to a remote age, free from legendary accretions, an Apostolic belief which affirms that the Incarnate Son consecrated by His presence the condition of departed souls.

## VI.

"THE special prominence given to the Ascension" in
the Apostles' Creed is, according to Professor Harnack,
"another deviation from the oldest teaching"; for "in
"the primitive tradition the Ascension had no separate
"place." "It is not quite certain," he adds, "that the
"writer of the Creed so conceived it, or that he did
"not rather intend to describe one single action by
"the three words 'risen,' 'ascended,' 'sitting'." It is
certain, however, that from the time of Rufinus they
have been otherwise understood; and Harnack's contention invites an examination into the grounds upon
which the Church regards the Ascension as an historical
event, distinct from the Resurrection, and preliminary
to the Session of our Lord at the right hand of God.

That the Ascension had no separate place in the
primitive tradition, appears, it is said, from the following considerations. (a) It is not mentioned by the
Synoptists, or by St Paul in his creed-like summary of
the Faith (1 Cor. xv. 3 ff.), or by the chief sub-apostolic
writers. (b) It is omitted in some of the oldest accounts,
which place the Session immediately after the Resurrection. (c) The interval between the Resurrection and
the Ascension is variously estimated by the earliest

authorities. It will be convenient to consider these points *seriatim*.

We have first the argument *ex silentio.* The Synoptists, we are told, know nothing of the Ascension; it is wanting in their Gospels. This statement needs some rectification. The first Gospel cannot fairly be said to omit the Ascension, for it does not carry the reader so far, stopping short with the meeting in Galilee. Whether the second Gospel omitted it may never be known, for if St Mark completed his work, the original ending is perhaps hopelessly lost. Nor is it certain that the Ascension is wanting in St Luke. After removing the interpolations from Luke xxiv. 50, 51, we still have the words διέστη ἀπ' αὐτῶν, καὶ αὐτοὶ ὑπέστρεψαν εἰς Ἰερουσαλὴμ μετὰ χαρᾶς μεγάλης. Διέστη may of course refer to a temporary parting, or to a permanent one not effected by an ascension; but the joyful return to Jerusalem is difficult to explain on either hypothesis. On the whole, then, the facts scarcely justify the assertion that the Ascension is "wanting in the first three "Gospels." But granting that it is, the silence of the Synoptists does not imply ignorance. There is another explanation which deserves to be considered. " The "Ascension," it has been said, "apparently did not lie "within the proper scope of the Gospels...its true "place was at the head of the Acts of the Apostles, as "the preparation for the Day of Pentecost, and thus "the beginning of the history of the Church[1]."

The silence of St Paul in 1 Cor. xv. is a still more precarious argument. The Apostle's purpose in that chapter is simply to establish the truth of the Resurrection, and it is idle to require him to step aside from

---

[1] *Notes on Select Readings* (App. to W. H.), p. 73.

his argument in order to mention the Ascension. Ἀπέ-
θανεν—ἐτάφη—ἐγήγερται—ὤφθη, form a series of statements essential to the matter in hand; the addition of
ἀνελήμφθη would have been at once superfluous and
misleading.

But the great sub-apostolic writers are also silent.
The relevance of this circumstance depends upon the
nature of their writings. What reason is there to expect
them to touch upon the subject of the Ascension?
Clement is almost exclusively concerned with the
maintenance of discipline. Ignatius, as the opponent
of Docetism, is chiefly interested in the Birth, the
Passion, and the Resurrection of the Lord. Polycarp
has left us only one short letter, which is taken up with
practical details. Nevertheless, Ignatius uses language
which seems to imply a belief in the Ascension[1], and
Polycarp, who quotes 1 Peter[2], could not have been
ignorant of St Peter's distinct reference to the event.

Thus the argument from the silence of early writers
is in itself insufficient to bear the weight of Dr Harnack's
conclusions. Moreover, it is only fair to set against the
silence of some writers the express statements of others
who fall within the same period. The present ending
to St Mark, which asserts the Ascension in the plainest
terms, belongs at the latest to the earlier sub-apostolic
age, and some cogent reasons have recently been produced for connecting it with the name of a personal
disciple of our Lord[3]. The fourth Gospel, which, even
if its Johannine authorship be not conceded, can hardly

---

[1] E.g. in *Magn.* 7 ἀφ' ἑνὸς πατρὸς
προελθόντα καὶ εἰς ἕνα ὄντα καὶ χωρή-
σαντα.

[2] *Philipp.* 1, 2 (*ter*), 5, 7, 8 (*bis*),
10.

[3] Aristion: see F. C. Conybeare
in *Expositor*, ser. iv. vol. viii. p.
241 ff., and the writer's *Gospel acc.
to St Mark*, p. ciii ff.

be placed later than the beginning of the second century, contains allusions to the Ascension which are the more significant because they are incidental (cc. vi. 62, xx. 17). If we may not assume that the Acts was the work of St Luke, or that the materials for the early chapters of that book were derived from original sources, the statements in cc. i. 9, ii. 33, 34, are at least earlier than the date of Polycarp's Epistle, which quotes c. ii. 24. The Epistle to the Ephesians assumes the fact of the Ascension (c. iv. 8—10); the Pastorals quote a primitive Christian hymn in which it is celebrated (1 Tim. iii. 16). Passages in the Epistles which speak of the Lord's Return may also fairly be claimed (e.g. 1 Thess. iv. 16, 2 Thess. i. 7), for the hope of a κατάβασις postulates an antecedent ἀνάβασις, without which it is inconceivable. On the whole it may confidently be maintained that the Christian literature of the century which followed the Ascension contains as many references and allusions to it as the position of that event in the Christian scheme and its relative importance in the estimation of the first age might have led us to expect.

But Professor Harnack proceeds to urge that "in "some of the oldest accounts the resurrection and the "sitting at the right hand of God are taken as parts of "the same act, without mention of any ascension." Let us interrogate one of these accounts. In Rom. viii. 34 St Paul writes: Χριστὸς Ἰησοῦς ὁ ἀποθανὼν μᾶλλον δὲ ἐγερθεὶς ἐκ νεκρῶν, ὅς ἐστιν ἐν δεξιᾷ τοῦ θεοῦ, ὃς καὶ ἐντυγχάνει ὑπὲρ ἡμῶν. Here are four well-marked links in a chain of facts—our Lord's death, resurrection, session, intercession. It is difficult to see why the second and the third, the Resurrection and the Session, should be taken as parts of the same act, when the first is clearly distinct. If the Ascension is not mentioned, it is implied in the Session, for it is contrary to the usage of the New Testament to interpret ἐγείρεσθαι of any exaltation beyond the mere recall from death. In other passages the ellipsis is equally easy to supply. Thus St Peter's words in Acts ii. 32 (τὸν Ἰησοῦν ἀνέστησεν ὁ θεὸς...τῇ δεξιᾷ οὖν τοῦ θεοῦ ὑψωθεὶς) are interpreted by 1 Pet. iii. 21, 22 (δι' ἀναστάσεως Ἰησοῦ Χριστοῦ, ὅς ἐστιν ἐν δεξιᾷ τοῦ θεοῦ, πορευθεὶς εἰς οὐρανόν). If in Eph. i. 20 the sequence ἐγείρας...καθίσας should be seized upon by a zealous advocate of the new teaching as a clear instance of the omission of the Ascension, he would presently find himself confronted by the appearance of the missing link in c. iv. 10 (ὁ ἀναβὰς ὑπεράνω πάντων τῶν οὐρανῶν). But a single instance from a later writer will suffice to shew the futility of this reasoning. Justin in one place brings the Crucifixion and the Ascension together (*dial.* 38 σταυρωθῆναι καὶ ἀναβεβηκέναι εἰς τὸν οὐρανόν). Will it be contended that he omits the Resurrection because he regarded it as 'part of the same act' with either the one or the other of the events which he mentions?

One argument remains. Opinion for a long time fluctuated with regard to the interval which elapsed between the Resurrection and the Ascension. This uncertainty is thought to shew the unsoundness of the received teaching. "It follows...that the differentiation" of the single fact "into several acts was the work of a "later time."

Let us examine the evidence. " In the Epistle of "Barnabas both resurrection and ascension happen in "one day." So Harnack. But the words are (c. 15): " We keep the eighth day for rejoicing, on which Jesus "both rose from the dead, and, after His manifestation, "ascended into heaven[1]." Barnabas seems to affirm that both the Resurrection and the Ascension occurred on the eighth day, or on a Sunday. But he does not even hint that they occurred on the same Sunday. Nor does his statement necessarily conflict with St Luke's (Acts i. 3 δι' ἡμερῶν τεσσεράκοντα ὀπτανόμενος). Undoubtedly it was a natural inference from St Luke's words that the Ascension took place on the fortieth day after the Resurrection; and this inference is already drawn by the author of the fifth book of the *Constitutions*[2], and since the fourth century has been sanctioned by the annual celebration of Holy Thursday. Yet the words of the Acts allow greater latitude, and would be satisfied if the Ascension could be shewn to have taken place on the following Sunday, the forty-third day after Easter. Indeed the Syriac *Doctrine of the Apostles* carries it forward to the fiftieth day, making it coincide with the Descent of the Holy Ghost[3]. This is clearly inconsistent with the Acts, but it lends some support to the statement of Barnabas that the Ascension occurred on the first day of the week.

But "other ancient witnesses give us yet a different "story, and make the interval eighteen months." Harnack omits to mention that these witnesses were certain Valentinians who sought by this arbitrary reckoning to bolster up their theory of the Pleroma[4]. A school of

[1] διὸ καὶ ἄγομεν τὴν ἡμέραν τὴν ὀγδόην εἰς εὐφροσύνην, ἐν ᾗ καὶ ὁ Ἰησοῦς ἀνέστη ἐκ νεκρῶν καὶ φανερωθεὶς ἀνέβη εἰς οὐρανούς.

[2] *Const. Ap.* v. 19 ἀπὸ τῆς πρώτης κυριακῆς ἀριθμήσαντες τεσσαράκοντα ἡμέρας, ἀπὸ κυριακῆς ἄχρι πέμπτης ἑορτάζετε τὴν ἑορτὴν τῆς ἀναλήψεως.

[3] Cureton, *Ancient documents*, pp. 24, 27.

[4] Iren. i. 3. 2 octodecim aeonas manifestari per id quod post resurrectionem a mortuis octodecim mensibus dicunt conuersatum eum cum discipulis. *Ib.* 30. 14 remoratum...eum post resurrectionem xviii mensibus, et sensibilitate in eum descendente didicisse quod liquidum est...et sic receptus est in caelum.

Ophites increased the interval to eleven or twelve years[1], probably on the strength of the tradition which represented the Apostles as having remained for the latter period at Jerusalem[2]. Even within the Church speculation sometimes ran riot upon this subject, and Eusebius in one place (*dem. ev.* viii. 2) suggests that our Lord's ministry lasted for the same number of years after the Passion as before it, three and a half years each way[3]. Such eccentricities shew that the statement of Acts i. 3 was not always accepted or regarded as fixing a limit of time ; but they certainly do not throw any reasonable doubt upon the fact of the Ascension, which is accepted without question by all Christian writers, Gnostic or Catholic, who refer to it at all.

To return to the Creed.   No doubt can be entertained as to the place of the words "ascendit in caelos" in the Old-Roman form.   In fact, no article in the Creed more certainly belongs to the earliest tradition.   Ἀνελήμφθη ἐν δόξῃ finds a place in the creed-like hymn already noted in 1 Tim. iii. 16.   Εἰς οὐρανοὺς ἀνῆλθεν stands in the confession of Aristides[4].   Irenaeus witnesses that the Church throughout the world believed in the assumption into heaven of the flesh (τὴν ἔνσαρκον εἰς τοὺς οὐρανοὺς ἀνάληψιν) of Jesus Christ[5].   Tertullian professes that He Who rose from the dead was "carried

---

[1] *Pistis Sophia*, p. 1 Schmidt, *gnostische Schriften*, p. 439. Cf. *Asc. Isai.* p. 43.

[2] So Apollonius *ap.* Euseb. *H. E.* v. 18.

[3] πρὸ μὲν γὰρ τοῦ πάθους ἐπὶ τρία καὶ ἥμισυ ἔτη τοῖς πᾶσιν ἑαυτὸν παρέχων μαθηταῖς τε καὶ τοῖς μὴ τοιούτοις ἀναγέγραπται...μετὰ δὲ τὴν ἐκ νεκρῶν ἀνάστασιν τὸν ἴσον, ὡς εἰκός, τῶν

ἐτῶν χρόνον τοῖς ἑαυτοῦ μαθηταῖς καὶ ἀποστόλοις συνῆν δι' ἡμερῶν τεσσαράκοντα ὀπτανόμενος αὐτοῖς καὶ συναλιζόμενος...ὡς γοῦν αἱ πράξεις τῶν ἀποστόλων περιέχουσιν, ὡς εἶναι ταύτην τὴν δηλουμένην τῆς προφητείας τῶν ἐτῶν ἑβδομάδα (cf. Dan. ix. 27).

[4] ed. Robinson, pp. 24, 110. Hennecke, p. 9.

[5] Iren. 1. 10. 1.

"up" (*ereptum*) or "taken back" (*receptum, resumtum*) into heaven[1]. None of these forms shews any trace of a confusion between the Resurrection and the Ascension, or of a suspicion that the latter was less truly matter of history than the former. It is evident, indeed, that from the first there were two ways of regarding the Ascension. It was either an ἀνάβασις or an ἀνάληψις, an ascent or an assumption. Both of these terms were suggested by passages in the LXX.—the first by Pss. xxiii (xxiv). 3 (τίς ἀναβήσεται εἰς τὸ ὄρος τοῦ κυρίου ;), lxvii (lxviii). 19 (ἀναβὰς εἰς ὕψος) ; the second by 4 Kings ii. 9—11 (ἀνελήμφθη Ἠλειού). The latter view, in which the mystical aspect of the event predominates, recommended itself to the writers of the Acts, the Marcan fragment, and the hymn cited in the Pastorals ; and it appears also in Irenaeus, Tertullian, and Origen, and in some of the later Eastern expositions of the Faith. But the great Eastern Creeds, and the Western Creeds with scarcely an exception, represent our Lord as having 'gone up to heaven,' using either ἀναβαίνειν (*ascendere*) or ἀνέρχεσθαι. These expressions, which emphasise the historical character of the mystery, viewing it from the standpoint of its earthly surroundings, rest upon equally good authority with the other (John vi. 62, xx. 17 ; Eph. iv. 10) ; and the Church almost from the first shewed a disposition to prefer them for symbolical purposes. Ἀνάληψις was capable of misinterpretation ; it will be remembered that it is used in a doubtfully orthodox sense by the Docetic author of the Petrine Gospel[2]. An assumption into heaven might mean

---

[1] *de uel. uirg.* 1, *de praescr.* 13 ; *adu. Prax.* 2.
[2] *Akhmîm Fragment*, p. 10. On the word see *Pss. of Solomon* (ed. Ryle and James), iv. 20, *n.*

nothing more than the return of the higher nature of Christ to the Father or the exaltation of His human spirit, and Irenaeus, it will have been observed, is careful to guard himself against these misconceptions by describing the assumption of Christ as ἔνσαρκος. It may have been for this reason that the Creeds, with remarkable unanimity, fell back upon the other group of expressions, which, while equally Scriptural, left no room for doubt. The original Roman Creed, so far as we can discover, used the unambiguous phrase[1]; and the suggestion that its authors possibly regarded *ascendit in caelos* as merely another presentation of *resurrexit a mortuis* is not justified by the arguments by which it has been supported. The legend which assigned the two clauses to two Apostles[2] is nearer to the truth than the latest criticism, in so far as the former emphasises what the latter fails to recognise, that the Resurrection and the Ascension are historically distinct although closely related events. This fact was present to the mind of the writer of the fourth Gospel when he represented the Lord as saying to the Magdalene after His resurrection, Οὔπω...ἀναβέβηκα[3], and it was certainly not hidden from the teachers of the Western Church, when towards the middle of the second century they confessed that Jesus Christ both "rose from the dead" and "ascended into heaven."

---

[1] *Ascendit* seems to be without variant; ἀναβάντα answers to it in Marcellus and the Athelstan Psalter, ἀνελθόντα in the St Gall and Corpus MSS.

[2] Hahn, p. 52: Thomas dixit... *resurrexit a mortuis.* Jacobus dixit *ascendit ad caelos.*

[3] John xx. 17.

## VII

THERE is another group of controverted points in the Apostles' Creed which remains to be examined. It belongs to the third paragraph of the Creed, and the three points it includes relate to the character and the privileges of the Church.

*Credo...sanctam ecclesiam.* So the Old Roman Creed was content to confess. "Holy Church," if not a New Testament phrase, is certainly in harmony with New Testament teaching (1 Pet. ii. 9, 1 Cor. iii. 17), and it appears in the earliest literature of the second century[1]. At Rome it must have been familiar before the middle of the second century; in Hermas the Church, an imposing figure in the imagery of the *Shepherd*, is thrice entitled ἡ ἁγία (*uis.* i. 1. 6, 3. 4; iv. 1. 3). Tertullian (*adu. Marc.* v. 4) quotes Marcion's text of Gal. iv. 27 in the form "quae est mater nostra in quam repromisimus "sanctam ecclesiam[2]." The words seem to bear witness that in Marcion's time persons who were admitted to the

---

[1] See e.g. Ign. *Trall.* 1 ἐκκλησίᾳ ἁγίᾳ τῇ οὔσῃ ἐν Τράλλεσιν, and the anti-Montanist writer Apollonius in Euseb. *H. E.* v. 18 ἔτι δὲ καὶ Θεμίσων ...ἐτόλμησε...βλασφημῆσαι...εἰς τὸν Κύριον καὶ τοὺς ἀποστόλους καὶ τὴν ἁγίαν ἐκκλησίαν.

[2] The same reading appears in Ephrem's commentary on the Pauline Epistles recently published in Latin by the Mechitarist fathers of San Lazzaro; cf. Harris, *Four Lectures on the Western Text*, p. 19 f.

communion of the Roman Church were required to confess their belief in the Holy Church. We may therefore
be fairly certain that *sanctam ecclesiam* stood in the
Roman Creed during Marcion's residence at Rome[1].

On the other hand, 'catholic' as a symbolical term is
neither Roman nor Western. Outside the Creed it is of
frequent use in Christian Latinity from the end of the
second century. Tertullian not only employs *catholicus*
freely, but combines it with *ecclesia* (*adu. Marc.* iv. 4), and
the translator of the Muratorian fragment has it in the
same connexion. Nevertheless *sanctam ecclesiam catholicam* does not appear in a Western Creed before the latter
part of the fifth century, and probably never made its way
into the true Creed of the Roman Church; when adopted
in Gaul, it was doubtless an importation from the East,
where its use was at this time all but universal[2]. The
absence from the Roman Creed of so ancient and
widespread a term may possibly have been due to the
comparative independence of the great Mother Church
of the West. She did not feel herself in need of the
support which the scattered Churches of the East derived from the thought of the solidarity of the Christian
brotherhood. It may be suspected that Rome was
never in hearty sympathy with the idea of the Church's
catholicity; when she borrowed the word, it was
narrowed in her use of it into a sense alien to that which
it had borne on the lips of the first teachers of the Faith.

---

[1] I.e. during the episcopate of
Anicetus (Iren. iii. 4. 3), or, roughly
speaking, in the sixth decade of the
second century.

[2] It is in the Creed expounded
by St Cyril of Jerusalem, *cat.*
xviii. 26, in that of the *Constitutions* (vii. 41 τῇ ἁγίᾳ καθολικῇ καὶ
ἀποστολικῇ ἐκκλησίᾳ), in the Epi-
phanian creeds, and finally in the
'Constantinopolitan' creed, where,
as in the Creed of the *Constitutions*,
it is supplemented by 'apostolic'
(εἰς μίαν ἁγίαν καθολικὴν καὶ ἀποστολικὴν ἐκκλησίαν).

'Catholic' is not a word of Biblical origin; καθολικός appears neither in the LXX. nor in the text of the New Testament[1]; its Latin representative finds no place in the Vulgate, or, apparently, in the older Latin versions. Yet the word lay ready for use in the pages of the later Greek writers, and had been adopted by Philo[2]. As applied to the Church, it meets us for the first time in the letters of Ignatius, who writes to the Smyrnaeans (c. 8), " Wheresoever Jesus Christ is, there is the Catholic "Church." It is singular that its next appearance is in the circular letter of the Church of Smyrna, addressed on occasion of the martyrdom of Polycarp "to all the " congregations (παροικίαις) of the holy and catholic "Church in every place[3]." The phrase is thus a true product of the sub-apostolic age; and if it gained admission into the Western Creed at a relatively late date, it can claim to have been known to the Churches of Asia Minor before the Roman Creed had taken its earliest form.

Professor Harnack, however, contends that the term " Catholic Church," as used in the fifth century, had drifted away from its original meaning. " Originally it " meant nothing more than the 'universal' Church, the " whole Christian community called of God on earth. " The idea of applying it to the concrete, visible Church " was not yet thought of....But after the end of the " second and the beginning of the third century, the word " 'Catholic' took a second meaning, which gradually " came to be regarded in the West as of equal authority

---

[1] Καθόλου occurs in Acts iv. 18; καθολικός only in the headings of the 'Catholic' Epistles as represented by the later uncial MSS. Comp. Westcott, *Epp. of St John*, p. xxviii.

[2] See Lightfoot's note on Ign. *Smyrn.* 8 (ii. p. 310).

[3] The word occurs thrice in this relatively short letter (Lightfoot, *l.c.*).

" with the first.    It described the visible, orthodox
" Churches which, under definite organisation, had
" grouped themselves round the Apostolic foundations,
" and especially round Rome, as distinguished from the
" heretical communities."

There are three points in this statement which
need separate examination.    In the first place we
are told that the Catholic Church, as conceived by
writers of the second century, was not a ' concrete, visible'
body.    It was, we must suppose, an invisible abstraction,
realised by a mental process, but possessing as yet no
tangible form.    This is true of the Church in the same
sense as it is true of every world-wide society which
cannot be presented to the eye in its completeness ; but
it is no less true of the later Catholic Church than of its
earliest beginnings.    On the other hand the units which
compose the Catholic Church were as concrete and visible
in the days of Ignatius as in those of Cyprian.    When
Ignatius argues that the Bishop is the centre of the
particular Church, as Jesus Christ is of the whole Society,
he certainly means by the Catholic Church the aggregate
of all the Christian congregations, which were visible
and concrete bodies.    It is difficult to discover any
essential difference between this conception and that
which prevailed after the second century.    " The Church
" is called 'Catholic'," writes Cyril of Jerusalem, " because
" she extends through the whole world, from one end of
" the earth to the other[1]."    The earliest expositions of
*catholicam* after its introduction into the Western Creed

---

[1] *catech*. xviii. 23 καθολικὴ μὲν
οὖν καλεῖται διὰ τὸ κατὰ πάσης εἶναι
τῆς οἰκουμένης ἀπὸ περάτων γῆς ἕως
περάτων. He adds other less perti-
nent reasons : (2) διὰ τὸ διδάσκειν
καθολικῶς καὶ ἀνελλιπῶς ἅπαντα...
(3) διὰ τὸ πᾶν γένος ἀνθρώπων εἰς
εὐσέβειαν ὑποτάσσειν...(4) διὰ τὸ
καθολικῶς ἰατρεύειν...ἅπαν τὸ τῶν
ἁμαρτιῶν εἶδος.

are entirely in harmony with this view. " What," asks a Gallican writer, " is the Catholic Church, but the people " who have been dedicated to God throughout the world? "As different members make up the completeness of the " human body, so a variety of races and nations, agreeing " in one faith, form the one body of Christ[1]." The Catholic Church as conceived by the teachers of the fourth and fifth centuries was neither more nor less concrete than the Church of the Ignatian age.

Harnack is on still more doubtful ground if he means to suggest that in the West the word 'Catholic' soon became the symbol of the organisation which grouped the Churches round the See of Rome, and ended in their subjection to the Papal supremacy. That the Churches of the West even in the second century had begun to look up to Rome with the reverence which was thought to be due to the foundation of St Peter and St Paul is familiar to every one who has read Irenaeus and Tertullian; "ad hanc enim ecclesiam propter potentiorem "principalitatem necesse est omnem convenire ecclesiam[2]," expresses the feeling of the Church of South Gaul about A.D. 180, whilst from Carthage at the end of the century there comes an equally clear note: " percurre ecclesias " apostolicas...si...Italiae adiaces, habes Romam, unde " nobis quoque auctoritas praesto est[3]." That this tendency existed is matter of fact; that it affected the sense of the word 'catholic,' or influenced its introduction into the Creed, has not been proved. Evidence is wanting

---

[1] S. Faustini *tract. de Symb.* (in Caspari *alte u. neue Quellen*, p. 272 sq.): quae est ecclesia catholica, nisi dicata Deo plebs per omnem diffusa mundum? nam sicut diuersa hominis membra, uariis ministeriis sibi congrua, capiti suo militant ac de se corpus integrum reddunt, sic et uariae gentes diuersaeque nationes in unam fidem conuenientes unum de se Christi corpus efficiunt.

[2] Iren. iii. 3. 2.

[3] Tertull. *de praescr.* 36.

to shew that Irenaeus and Tertullian, Cyprian and Augustine, understood the Catholic Church to mean the aggregate of the Churches which recognised the supremacy of Rome. The phrase came from the East, where the influence of the Roman Bishops was less directly felt than in Africa and Gaul; it was used by Western writers to comprehend the whole Christian brotherhood throughout the world; the earliest expositors of the Apostles' Creed manifest no desire to employ it as a vehicle for enforcing Roman claims. Under these circumstances it is unreasonable to prejudice the phrase by reading into it a tendency which it does not appear to have reflected until a much later age[1].

One point remains in Harnack's indictment. He reminds us that the word 'catholic' became after the second century a synonym for 'orthodox,' and that the Catholic Church was limited to those Christian societies which were regarded as retaining the Apostles' faith. Here the Berlin Professor is on solid ground. The growth of heresy and the gradual separation of heretical minorities from the great body of the faithful, led to a secondary application of the word 'catholic.' Catholics were contrasted with heretics, the Catholic Church with the sects which had parted from it. Perhaps the earliest genuine example of this change is to be found in the Muratorian fragment, which excludes from

---

[1] Harnack selects Cyprian as a conspicuous leader in the movement by which "the idea [of catholicity] was developed in this direction." The selection of Cyprian's name will seem unfortunate to those who remember his independent attitude towards Stephen. Cyprian's idea of catholicity is that of an organic union of Churches, resting on the oneness of the Episcopate which represents Christ. Comp. *ep*. 66. 8 scire debes episcopum in ecclesia esse et ecclesiam in episcopo...ecclesia quae catholica una est, scissa non [est] neque diuisa. sed [est] utique conexa et cohaerentium sibi inuicem sacerdotum glutine copulata. This is only the view of Ignatius more fully worked out. See Archbp Benson's *Cyprian*, p. 186 ff.

the canon certain heretical apocrypha "quae in catho-
"licam ecclesiam recipi non potest." As we proceed, the
secondary sense becomes frequent. The letter of Pope
Cornelius († 252), which has been preserved by Eusebius
(*H. E.* vi. 43), complains that his rival Novatian was
ignorant that 'a Catholic Church could have but one
'Bishop.' 'Who are you?' the martyr Pionius was
asked by the examining magistrate. 'A Christian.' 'Of
'what Church?' 'Of the Church Catholic[1].' "When you
"are abroad in foreign cities," Cyril charges his catechumens, "do not enquire simply for the Church, for the
"heretical sects venture to call their dens by that name;
"but ask for the Catholic Church[2]." St Pacian, when
the Novatianists asked why he called himself a Catholic
and was not content to be known as a Christian, replied
"'Christian' is my name, 'Catholic' my surname; the latter
"distinguishes me from others who bear the same name,
"but are not of the same family[3]." This limitation

[1] Ruinart, *act. mart. sinc.* p. 191
post haec Polemon...ait ad Pionium,
*Quis uocaris?* Pionius ait, *Christianus.* Polemon : *Cuius ecclesiae?*
Pionius ait, *Catholicae.* The Bollan-
dist Acts (Febr. i. p. 44) add "nulla
est enim est alia apud Christum."
The Acts represent Polemo as addressing similar questions to two
other martyrs. Pionius suffered in
the Decian persecution, March 12,
250. The Acts have survived only
in a Latin dress, but the story of the
examination has the ring of genuine-
ness, and is given in substantially
the same form by both recensions.

[2] *catech.* xviii. 26 κἄν ποτε ἐπι-
δημῇς ἐν πόλεσι, μὴ ἁπλῶς ἐξέταζε
ποῦ τὸ κυριακόν ἐστι (καὶ γὰρ αἱ
λοιπαὶ τῶν ἀσεβῶν αἱρέσεις κυριακὰ
τὰ ἑαυτῶν σπήλαια καλεῖν ἐπιχει-
ροῦσι), μηδὲ ποῦ ἐστιν ἁπλῶς ἡ ἐκκλη-
σία· ἀλλὰ ποῦ ἐστιν ἡ καθολικὴ

ἐκκλησία. τοῦτο γὰρ ἴδικὸν ὄνομα
τυγχάνει τῆς ἁγίας ταύτης καὶ μητρὸς
ἡμῶν ἁπάντων, κ.τ.λ.
[3] *ad Symphr. Novat. ep.* i. 3, 4.
The Novatianists urged that the name
was not primitive : "sed sub apostolis,
inquies, nemo catholicus uocabatur.
esto, sic fuerit, uel illud indulge (*fors.*
*leg.* indulgeo). cum post apostolos
haereses exstitissent...nonne cognomen suum plebs apostolica postula-
bat?...ego forte ingressus populosam
urbem hodie, cum Marcionitas...et
ceteros eiusmodi comperissem qui se
Christianos uocarent, quo cognomine
congregationem meae plebis agnos-
cerem, nisi catholica diceretur?...
'Christianus' mihi nomen est, 'catholicus' uero cognomen; illud me
nuncupat, istud ostendit; hoc probor,
inde significor." Pacian was Bp of
Barcelona in the second half of the
fourth century.

of the magnificent phrase of Ignatius was doubtless deplorable, but it was necessary. Everywhere in the third century there were Christians and Christians; the Churches which held to the Apostolic tradition were parted by an impassable gulf from the disciples of Valentinus and Basilides; yet the latter recognised the Gospels, and passed as members of Christ. But 'Catholics' they could not be called, for heresy was essentially partial and local, and limited to the few[1]. Nothing was more natural than that the name which did not fit heretics should become the distinctive property of the majority, and thus the mark of orthodoxy which attached itself to tenets, societies, individuals, and even buildings which were used in the worship of the Apostolic Church.

It may readily be admitted that this secondary meaning was present to the thoughts of the generation which defined the Holy Church of the Western Creed to be 'catholic.' *Catholicam*, as understood in the fifth century, was exclusive as well as comprehensive; it embraced all Christian communities which held fast by the Apostolic doctrine and discipline, but shut the door against those who rejected either. Neither the Arian nor the Donatist could claim to belong to a Church which was defined as Catholic. Possibly it was the exclusiveness of the term quite as much as its comprehensiveness which commended it to the post-Augustinian Church. "Know," writes Nicetas, "that

---

[1] Lightfoot, *l.c.* (p. 311): "The truth was the same everywhere, 'quod semper, quod ubique, quod ab omnibus.' The heresies were partial, scattered, localized, isolated." The early heretics gloried in being the minority, and not of the vulgar herd of Churchmen; cf. Iren. iii. 15. 2 eos qui sunt ab ecclesia...' communes ecclesiasticos' ipsi dicunt.

"this one Catholic Church is planted in all the world,
"and be sure that you adhere stedfastly to her com-
"munion. There are, it is true, other Churches falsely
"so called, but you have nothing in common with them ;
"heretical or schismatical bodies have ceased to be 'holy'
"Churches, for their faith and practice differ from that
"which Christ commanded and His Apostles delivered[1]."

Harnack congratulates himself that the Protestant
Churches of Germany replaced 'Catholic' by 'Christian,'
in their version of the Apostles' Creed. "The Church
"of the Reformation could not," he says, "consent to
"retain an epithet" which had received an interpretation foreign to her conceptions. As a matter of fact,
one great 'Church of the Reformation' retains it to this
day. Our English Reformers ridiculed the absurdity of
identifying the Catholic Church with a single branch of
the Church[2]. But their resistance to the Roman claims
did not suggest to them the expediency of abandoning
the term which had been thus abused. It remains in
the English Prayer-Book as a witness to the continuity
of the Reformed Church in England with the Church of
the early centuries. In the midst of the thousand
divisions of Christendom it points to the organic unity
of the true Body of Christ. Among the cries which
proclaim the advent of an 'undenominational' and 'un-
sectarian' Christianity it witnesses to the preciousness of
a definite faith.

[1] Caspari, *anecdota*, p. 357 : scito unam hanc esse ecclesiam catholicam in omni orbe terrae constitutam, cuius communionem debes firmiter retinere. sunt quidem et aliae pseudo-ecclesiae, sed nihil tibi commune cum illis...quia iam desinunt istae ecclesiae esse sanctae, siquidem daemoniacis deceptae doctrinis aliter credunt, aliter agunt quam Christus dominus mandauit, quam apostoli tradiderunt.

[2] Cf. e.g. Nowell's Catechism (ed. Parker Soc., p. 55): dum uniuersitatem Ecclesiae...nomine unius gentis apposito contrahunt...insanire iudico, ut qui contraria et inter se pugnantia uno spiritu uolaunt et pronuncient.

# VIII.

IF the phrase 'Catholic Church' came into the Apostles' Creed from an Eastern source, the words which follow are undoubtedly Western. Greek versions of the Creed translate them by ἁγίων κοινωνίαν, 'a joint participation in holy things[1].' This meaning is indeed assigned to the Latin words by some writers of the eleventh and twelfth centuries. Peter Abelard, after offering other explanations, adds, "Possumus et *sanctorum* "dicere neutraliter, id est, sanctificati panis et uini in " sacramentum altaris[2]"; and a Norman-French version, written at the end of the first quarter of the twelfth century, renders: "la communiun des seintes choses[3]." But the age which introduced the words into the Creed shews no knowledge of this interpretation. The idea was familiar, but it was expressed by another Latin phrase—*communio sacramentorum*, which is frequent in the writings of Augustine[4]. In *sanctorum communio* the adjective is masculine; the words mean the "communing"

---

[1] Or τὴν τῶν ἁγίων κοινωνίαν, or τῶν ἁγίων τὴν κοιν.; one MS. has ἁγίαν κοιν. See Heurtley, p. 82; Hahn, p. 32 *n*.

[2] *expos. in symb. ap.*, Migne, *P. L.* clxxviii. 629. Ivo of Chartres (*ib.* clxii. 606) strives to combine this interpretation with that which makes *sanctorum* masculine: "id est, eccle-

siasticorum sacramentorum ueritatem cui communicauerunt sancti."

[3] Heurtley, p. 93; Hahn, p. 83.

[4] E.g. *serm.* 214 malos...tolerat in communione sacramentorum. *c. ep. Parmenian.* ii. 8 communione sacramentorum, sicut dicitis, contaminantur.

or "communion of Saints," as the English Creeds have rendered them from the fourteenth century[1]. The conception
became prominent, as Harnack justly remarks, during the
Donatist controversy[2]. The Donatists declaimed against
a Church in which a "communio malorum," a joint participation in sacraments of the evil and the good, was
not only permitted but enforced. "What communion,"
they asked with St Paul, "hath light with darkness[3]?"
Augustine replied that though in the Catholic Church
the evil were mingled with the good, and the Church
was to that extent a mixed body, there was within her a
true *communio sanctorum,* in which the evil have no part,
and which is not impaired by their presence. The conception is therefore Augustinian, yet it did not claim a
place in the African Creed, or perhaps in any Creed,
until after Augustine's death. As a symbolical phrase
*sanctorum communionem* meets us first in a group of
homilies on the Creed of somewhat uncertain date, but,
with one doubtful exception, not earlier than the close
of the fifth century. It will be of interest to collect the
interpretations put upon the new clause in these earliest
expositions. The homily attributed to Nicetas asks,
"What is the Church, but the congregation of all
"saints? Patriarchs, prophets, apostles, martyrs, all the
"just who have been, are, or shall be, are one Church,
"because, sanctified by one faith and life, marked by
"One Spirit, they constitute one body. Believe, then,

---

[1] Comp. Heurtley, pp. 96—101.
[2] The phrase itself is earlier, for
it occurs in the Acts of the Council
of Nîmes, A.D. 394: Hefele, ii. 58
"sanctorum communione speciem
simulatae religionis [sibi] impri-
munt." The reference is to certain
Manicheans who passed themselves

off as Catholic presbyters and deacons
and procured Church communion.
[3] See Aug. *c. ep. Parmenian.*
ii. 37, and comp. *de bapt. c. Donatist.*
ii. 8, v. 38 (*ad fin.*), vii. 49 (malorum
communione quasi contagione bonos
perire contendunt).

"that in this one Church you will attain the communion
"of Saints[1]." Similarly, the sermon numbered 241 in
the appendix to Augustine explains the communion of
Saints as the result of the holiness of the Church and
of her common faith[2]. These two homilies reflect more
or less faithfully the original meaning of the phrase, for
they evidently take the words as they stand in the
Creed to be an answer to the false puritanism which was
dissatisfied with the *permixtum corpus* of the Catholic
Church; the Donatist controversy is still well in sight.
But *sanctorum communionem* lent itself readily to another
interpretation, which circumstances made especially
welcome towards the end of the century. There was a
growing tendency to limit the title of 'Saint' to the
departed, especially to martyrs; and this meaning was
eagerly read into the new clause by the Church of South
Gaul. In the southern dioceses of Gaul the party of
Vigilantius was still active[3], and the clause when thus interpreted was found to offer a valuable basis for teaching
on the subject of the *cultus* of the holy dead. Two remarkable instances survive. A homily, attributed with much
probability to Faustus, Bishop of Riez, exhorts[4], "Let us

---

[1] Caspari, *anecdota*, i. p. 355 sq.
ecclesia quid aliud quam sanctorum
omnium congregatio? ab exordio
enim saeculi siue patriarchae...siue
prophetae siue apostoli siue martyres
siue ceteri iusti qui fuerunt, qui
sunt, qui erunt, una ecclesia sunt,
quia una fide et conuersatione sanctificati, uno Spiritu signati, unum
corpus effecti sunt...ergo in hac una
ecclesia crede te communionem con-
secuturum esse sanctorum.

[2] The words are: "credentes ergo
sanctam ecclesiam catholicam, sanctorum habentes communionem, quia
ubi est fides sancta ibi est et sancta
communio," &c.

[3] See the evidence collected in
Caspari, *alte u. neue Quellen*, p.
274 ff. (*n.* 141).

[4] Caspari, *anecdota*, i. p. 338 credamus et *sanctorum communionem*, sed
sanctos non tam pro Dei parte, quam
pro Dei honore ueneremur...colamus
in sanctis timorem et amorem Dei,
non diuinitatem Dei; colamus me-
rita, non quae de proprio habent sed
quae accipere pro deuotione merue-
runt. digne itaque uenerandi sunt,
dum nobis Dei cultum et futurae
uitae desiderium contemptu mortis
insinuant. Faustus uses the phrase
in his *de Sp. s.* i. 2. (I owe the
reference to Rev. A. E. Burn.)

"believe in *the communion of Saints*, not as though they "shared the prerogatives of God, but for the honour of "God; let us do homage to the fear and love of God mani- "fested in them; they are worthy of our veneration, inas- "much as by their contempt for death they induce in us "a spirit of devotion to God and of eager longing for "the life to come." The moderation of this language is worthy of all praise; but another Gallican homily, which adopts the same interpretation of the words of the Creed, is less tolerant: "This clause," the writer exclaims, "shuts "the mouths of those who blasphemously refuse to "honour the ashes of the Saints and friends of God, and "who do not hold that the glorious memory of the "blessed martyrs is to be cherished by doing honour "to their tombs; such persons are false to their "Creed, and have given the lie to the promise which "they made to Christ at the font[1]." This extravagance was due to local and temporary causes, and disappeared with them; but wherever the new clause travelled, the tendencies of the age secured the transmission with it of the later interpretation. Thus another of the homilies on the Creed falsely attributed to Augustine (App. *Serm.* 242), which seems to have been authorised in some Gallican dioceses for use at the *traditio symboli*[2], defines the communion of Saints to be "the association and "partnership in hope by which we are bound to the "Saints who have departed in the faith we have em- "braced"; whilst a third (*Serm.* 240) explains it to mean that "whereas in this life each believer has only an

---

[1] Caspari, *alte u. neue Quellen*, p. 273 sq. "illos hic sententia ista confundit qui sanctorum et amicorum Dei cineres non in honore debere esse blasphemant, qui beatorum martyrum gloriosam memoriam sa- crorum reuerentia monumentorum colendam esse non credunt. in symbolum praeuaricati sunt et Christo in fonte mentiti sunt."

[2] It is worked into the *missale Gallicanum uetus* (Muratori ii. 720 c).

" individual share in the gifts of the Spirit, in eternity
" they will be the common property of all, since each
" Saint will then find in others what he lacks in him-
" self[1]."

Professor Harnack is disposed to connect the introduction of the words into the Creed with the growing
*cultus* of the Saints[2]. The evidence is scanty, but upon
the whole we may hesitate to accept the view that
*sanctorum communionem* was added in the interests of
the Church party opposed to Vigilantius. Can it be
supposed that if the Bishops of South Gaul had desired
to insert a clause in the Creed with this object in view,
they would have selected so ambiguous a phrase?
And if this had been the original sense of the words
as they stood in the Creed, is it probable that it
would have been set aside by later writers in favour
of a more spiritual and liberal interpretation? These
considerations incline us to regard the explanation
offered by Nicetas and by the Pseudo-Augustine of
*Serm.* 241 as representing the original acceptation of
the clause. It was anti-Donatist, not anti-Vigilantian;
the use to which it was turned by Faustus and his
successors in South Gaul was an afterthought. We
take *sanctorum communionem* as expository of *sanctam*

---

[1] *Serm.* 242 *sanctorum communionem:* id est, cum illis sanctis qui in hac
quam suscepimus fide defuncti sunt,
societate et spei communione tene-
amur. 240 *s. c.*; quia dona S.
Spiritus licet in hac uita diuersa sint
in singulis in aeternitate tamen erunt
communia in uniuersis, ut quod
quisque sanctorum minus habuit in
se, hoc in aliena uirtute parti-
cipet.

[2] His words are: "We shall have

to consider it as highly probable that
the words in question were actually
taken to mean 'communion with the
martyrs and the chosen saints.' Thus
they were, to begin with, a continu-
ation and not a mere explanation of
the phrase 'Holy Catholic Church.'"
"A good and fitting interpretation—
which still was not the primitive
meaning of the clause *in the Creed*—
was to be found in Augustine."

*ecclesiam,* and not as a new article of faith. In some forms of the legend which distributes the articles of the Creed among the Apostles, the two clauses are assigned to the same Apostle[1]. A later conception of the meaning changed this order, and the 'Communion of Saints' was either linked to the 'Forgiveness of Sins' as the first of the privileges of the Catholic Church, or treated as a separate article. The English Reformers reverted to the original connexion. "Now would I hear thee tell," asks the master in Nowell's Catechism, "why after the Holy "Church thou immediately addest that we believe in "the Communion of Saints"; and the scholar replies, "Because these two belong all to one thing, and are "very fitly matched and agreeing together; for this "parcel (*pars*) doth somewhat more plainly express the "conjoining and society that is among the members of "the Church, than which there can none be nearer[2]."

There is of course no reason why this "conjoining "and society" should be limited to the living members of the Church. The interpretation which Faustus and his age assigned to the Communion of Saints erred by excluding the living, not by including the departed. The Church had from the most primitive times recognised the union of the dead members of Christ with the living[3]. But the primitive Church did not confuse saintliness with sinlessness, or narrow the Communion of Saints to a recognition of the honour due to the holy

---

[1] Thus, in Ps.-Aug. *Serm.* 240 both the clauses are assigned to St Matthew; but in *Serm.* 241 and in *scarapsus* of Priminius (c. A.D. 750), while *sanctam ecclesiam catholicam* falls to Simon Zelotes, *sanctorum communionem, remissionem peccatorum* is allotted to Judas Ἰακώβου.

In the Bangor book *s. c.* follows *abremissa peccatorum*; one or two late writers treat it as a separate article.

[2] ed. Parker Soc., p. 173 f.

[3] See e.g. Heb. xii. 22, 23 προσ-εληλύθατε...πνεύμασι δικαίων τετε-λειωμένων.

dead, or of the hope of blissful reunion with them in a future state. Nor has it been proved that the words were added to the Creed by persons who attached to them no larger or more practical significance. In England, at least, the Augustinian interpretation is traditional. The Sarum *ordo ad uisitandum infirmum* directs the parish priest in examining the sick lay-member of the Church upon his faith to say, "Dearest brother, dost thou believe "…in the Communion of Saints, that is, that all men "who live in charity are partakers of all the gifts of "grace which are dispensed in the Church, and that all "who are in fellowship with the just here in the life of "grace, are in fellowship with them in glory[1]"? There is no material difference between this explanation and that which has prevailed in the English Church since the Reformation.

[1] Maskell, *mon. rit.* i. p. 76.

## IX.

*Carnis resurrectionem*, the last article in the Old
Roman Creed, is a form of words which, as Professor
Harnack contends, is neither Pauline nor Johannine.
Indeed it appears to conflict with the plain teaching both
of the Pauline Epistles and the fourth Gospel; for does
not St Paul write, " Flesh and blood cannot inherit the
" Kingdom of God"; and does not St John represent our
Lord as having said, " It is the spirit that quickeneth, the
" flesh profiteth nothing[1]"?   Hence it is clear that "in her
" conception of the resurrection and the life everlasting
" as the 'resurrection of the flesh,' the post-apostolic
" Church overstepped the line commonly observed in
" the oldest preaching."  This statement is more guarded
than some others with which we have had to deal, but it
conveys an impression which a careful examination will
considerably modify.

Let it be admitted at once that the form in which
this article is cast in the Western Creed is not Biblical,
unless it may claim the authority of Job xix. 26, where
Clement of Rome reads ἀναστήσεις τὴν σάρκα μου[2], or of

[1] 1 Cor. xv. 50 σὰρξ καὶ αἷμα
βασιλείαν θεοῦ κληρονομῆσαι οὐ δύνα-
ται. John vi. 63 τὸ πνεῦμά ἐστιν τὸ
ζωοποιοῦν, ἡ σὰρξ οὐκ ὠφελεῖ οὐδέν.

[2] Clem. 1 *Cor.* 26 καὶ πάλιν Ἰὼβ
λέγει Καὶ ἀναστήσεις τὴν σάρκα μου

ταύτην τὴν ἀναντλήσασαν ταῦτα
πάντα.   The LXX. has ἀναστήσαι
τὸ δέρμα μου (עוֹרִי) τὸ ἀναντλοῦν
ταῦτα (אAℵᶜˑᵃ read σῶμα for δέρμα:
O. L. renderings are *cutis*, *pellis*,
*corium*, *corpus*; the Latin Clement,

Psalm xvi. 9—a passage applied in the New Testament only to the resurrection of Christ[1]. In its references to the general resurrection the New Testament distinctly inclines to the phrase ἀνάστασις νεκρῶν. St Paul speaks of a resurrection of the body (Rom. viii. 11, 1 Cor. xv. 44[2]), but not of a resurrection of the flesh: and it is easy to understand that his depreciatory use of σάρξ may have led him to shrink from the latter phrase. As for St John, Harnack's reference is scarcely to the point; the words of Christ in John vi. 63 merely deny that the flesh has of itself any quickening or vitalising power. The Evangelist whose keynote is the Incarnation of the Logos might not have been unwilling to carry the thought of the flesh into the future life of men. Still there is no evidence that this was done either by St John or by any writer of the Apostolic age.

But if the phrase does not appear within the limits of the Canon, " we can hardly doubt that from the very " earliest times the resurrection of the flesh was preached "by a few Christians, but it was not a universal doctrine." It would have been more exact to say that while the doctrine was in substance universally taught, the phrase seems to have been unknown in the earliest times. Barnabas (5. 6) clings to the New Testament form, ἡ ἐκ νεκρῶν ἀνάστασις; and in his classical passage on the Resurrection (1 *Cor.* 24 ff.) Clement of Rome does not speak of an ἀνάστασις σαρκός, although, as we have seen, he quotes Job xix. 26 in a translation which

---

*Anecdota Mareds.* ii. p. 27, gives *corpus*). Τὴν σάρκα seems to have arisen from מִבְּשָׂרִי in the next clause, where the LXX. differs considerably from the Heb.

[1] Ps. xv (=xvi). 9 ἔτι δὲ καὶ ἡ σάρξ μου κατασκηνώσει ἐπ᾽ ἐλπίδι, cited in

Acts ii. 25—31 (cf. xiii. 35—37).

[2] ὁ ἐγείρας ἐκ νεκρῶν Χριστὸν Ἰησοῦν ζωοποιήσει καὶ τὰ θνητὰ σώματα ὑμῶν. σπείρεται σῶμα ψυχικόν, ἐγείρεται σῶμα πνευματικόν · εἰ ἔστιν σῶμα ψυχικόν, ἔστιν καὶ πνευματικόν.

directly suggests it.　In Ignatius at length we meet with a categorical assertion of the resurrection of the flesh, but he asserts it only in reference to the Flesh of Christ. Ignatius had a special reason for insisting on the resurrection of the Flesh of the Lord, for this truth was essential to his case against the Docetic teachers of his age.　The Gospel, he urges, represents the Lord not only as having come in the flesh and suffered in the flesh, but as having risen again in the same flesh in which He was crucified.　'I know and believe,' Ignatius testifies, 'that even after the Resurrection He was in 'the flesh...the Resurrection was, like the Passion, in 'the flesh as well as in the spirit[1].'　Other writers of the same period extend this way of speaking to the general resurrection.　Docetism denied the reality of the general resurrection, as well as of the Resurrection of Christ.　The tendency had begun to reveal itself before the close of the Canon, and the Pastoral Epistles speak of those who asserted that the resurrection was "past "already" (2 Tim. ii. 18), regarding it no doubt as a purely spiritual change.　In the second century this heresy reappeared in an aggravated form.　Writing to Philippi shortly after the martyrdom of Ignatius, Polycarp denounces a party who denied the resurrection and the future judgement, coupling them with those who refused to admit the reality of the Incarnation[2].　"They

---

[1] *Smyrn.* 3 ἐγὼ γὰρ καὶ μετὰ τὴν ἀνάστασιν ἐν σαρκὶ αὐτὸν οἶδα καὶ πιστεύω ὄντα· καὶ ὅτε πρὸς τοὺς περὶ Πέτρον ἦλθεν ἔφη αὐτοῖς Λάβετε, ψηλαφήσατέ με, καὶ ἴδετε ὅτι οὐκ εἰμὶ δαιμόνιον ἀσώματον· καὶ εὐθὺς αὐτοῦ ἥψαντο, καὶ ἐπίστευσαν κραθέντες τῇ σαρκὶ αὐτοῦ καὶ τῷ αἵματι ...μετὰ δὲ τὴν ἀνάστασιν καὶ συνέφαγεν αὐτοῖς καὶ συνέπιεν ὡς σαρκικός. *ib.*

12 πάθει τε καὶ ἀναστάσει σαρκικῇ τε καὶ πνευματικῇ.

[2] *Philipp.* 7 πᾶς γὰρ ὃς ἂν μὴ ὁμολογῇ Ἰησοῦν Χριστὸν ἐν σαρκὶ ἐληλυθέναι ἀντίχριστός ἐστιν...καὶ ὃς ἂν μεθοδεύῃ τὰ λόγια τοῦ κυρίου πρὸς τὰς ἰδίας ἐπιθυμίας καὶ λέγει μήτε ἀνάστασιν μήτε κρίσιν, οὗτος πρωτότοκός ἐστι τοῦ Σατανᾶ. Comp. Hippol. v. 8 ἐξαλοῦνται ἐκ τῶν μνημείων οἱ νεκροί·

"teach," Justin tells Trypho, "that there is no resurrec-
"tion of the dead, but their souls are received at death
"into heaven[1]." But the denial was not absolute ; the
Docetic Gnostics described by Tertullian (*de resurr.
carnis* 19) found a place in their systems for the resurrection of the dead, identifying it either with Baptism,
or with the spiritual awakening which they supposed to
follow the acceptance of their principles. "Resurrectio-
"nem mortuorum in imaginariam significationem dis-
"torquent," is the complaint of Tertullian. The faithful
were deceived by the vehemence of their protestations :
"Woe," they cried, "to him who has not risen again in
"the flesh," meaning, 'Woe to him who has not become
'acquainted with our gnosis[2].' But Gnostic subtilty could
find no way to evade the plain meaning of the phrase
*carnis resurrectio.* This form of words was non-scriptural,
but it was necessary in order to safeguard scriptural truth ;
and the Church of the second century did not hesitate
to adopt it[3], just as two centuries afterwards the Church
of the Nicene age accepted the Homoousion in order to
protect another fundamental doctrine of the Catholic faith.

τουτέστιν, ἐκ τῶν σωμάτων τῶν χοϊκῶν
ἀναγεννηθέντες πνευματικοί, οὐ σαρ-
κικοί.

[1] *dial.* 80 οἳ καὶ λέγουσιν μὴ εἶναι
νεκρῶν ἀνάστασιν ἀλλὰ ἅμα τῷ ἀπο-
θνήσκειν τὰς ψυχὰς αὐτῶν ἀναλαμβά-
νεσθαι εἰς τὸν οὐρανόν. Comp. Iren.
v. 31. 1.

[2] "'Uae (inquiunt) qui non in
hac carne resurrexerit,'ne statim illos
percutiant si resurrectionem statim
abnuerint. tacite autem secundum
conscientiam suam hoc sentiunt :
' Uae qui non, dum in hac carne
est, cognouerit arcana haeretica':
hoc est enim apud illos resurrectio."

[3] Comp. Justin, *dial.* 80 ἐγὼ δὲ
καὶ εἴ τινές εἰσιν ὀρθογνώμονες κατὰ

πάντα Χριστιανοί...σαρκὸς ἀνάστασιν
γενήσεσθαι ἐπιστάμεθα. He adds,
καὶ χίλια ἔτη ἐν Ἱερουσαλήμ, but
this avowal of chiliastic views does
not impair his testimony to the orthodox character of the phrase
σαρκὸς ἀνάστασις. Irenaeus (I. 10.
1) attributes to the whole Church
the belief that Christ shall come ἐπὶ
τὸ...ἀναστῆσαι πᾶσαν σάρκα πάσης
ἀνθρωπότητος. It formed part of
Tertullian's Rule of Faith (*de uel.
uirg.* 1 uenturum iudicare uiuos et
mortuos per carnis etiam resurrectionem): cf. *de praescr.* 13 facta...
resuscitatione, cum carnis restitutione.

The Docetic party fell back upon the passage in St Paul which is now produced by Professor Harnack. The words 'Flesh and blood cannot inherit the king-'dom of God' were quoted, Irenaeus tells us, by all the heretical sects against the teaching of the Church[1]. But she had her answer ready. Irenaeus explains that the Apostle speaks of the flesh considered apart from the Spirit, i.e. human nature unsanctified and unrenewed[2]. Tertullian points out that St Paul does not say, 'The 'flesh shall not rise,' but that it shall not enter the king-dom till a change has passed over it[3]. Origen meets Celsus, who ridiculed the Church-doctrine of the resur-rection of the flesh, with the rejoinder, "Neither we "nor the sacred Scriptures assert that those who are "long dead shall live again in their flesh, as it was, "without having undergone any change for the better[4]." Notwithstanding characteristic differences, these answers came practically to the same point. The Church does not affirm what St Paul denies. The 'resurrection of 'the flesh' as it is taught in the Creed does not exclude the thought of the great change which, as the Apostle teaches, must pass over the material part of human nature before it can be admitted into the perfect life.

Nevertheless it must be confessed that the phrase which was forced upon the Church by the sophistries of a false gnosis was used by some of the orthodox in a

[1] v. 9. 1 id est quod ab omnibus haereticis profertur in amentiam suam.

[2] *ib.* 3 ἐβόησε μὴ δύνασθαι τὴν σάρκα καθ᾽ ἑαυτὴν...βασιλείαν κληρονομῆσαι θεοῦ.

[3] *de res. carn.* 50 resurgunt itaque ex aequo omnis caro et sanguis in qualitate sua. sed quorum est adire regnum Dei, induere oportebit uim incorruptibilitatis et immortalitatis,

sine qua regnum Dei adire non possunt.

[4] *c. Cels.* v. 18 οὔτε μὲν οὖν ἡμεῖς οὔτε τὰ θεῖα γράμματα αὐταῖς φησι σαρξί, μηδεμίαν μεταβολὴν ἀνειλη-φυίαις τὴν ἐπὶ τὸ βέλτιον, ζήσεσθαι τοὺς πάλαι ἀποθανόντας ἀπὸ τῆς γῆς ἀναδύντας· ὁ δὲ Κέλσος συκοφαντεῖ ἡμᾶς ταῦτα λέγων. Origen proceeds to quote St Paul.

sense which was really un-Pauline and unprimitive. It
was innocent and right so long as it was turned against
the Docetic denial of a true resurrection of the body
or used in the interests of vigilance and purity. We
can still feel the force of the Pseudo-Clement's appeal :
" Let none of you say that this flesh is not judged
" nor rises again. Consider : wherein were ye saved,
" wherein did ye recover your sight? was it not in
" this flesh? We ought, then, to guard the flesh as
" a temple of God ; for as in the flesh ye were called,
" in the flesh ye shall also come..., in this flesh ye
" shall receive your reward[1]." Nor has the warning in
Hermas lost its importance: " See that the thought do
" not enter thy heart that this flesh of thine is perish-
" able... if thou defile the flesh, thou shalt not live[2]."
But Tertullian carries us into another region of thought
when he writes, "Resurget igitur caro, et quidem omnis
" et quidem ipsa et quidem integra[3]." Here the interest is no longer ethical, and a phrase which was
chiefly valuable as a protest against a false spirituality
is pressed to the length of a crude materialism. The
evil was one which was certain to spread, and it was
not without cause that Origen complained of the views
entertained by certain otherwise excellent Christians
who imagined that the identical bones and flesh and
blood which were buried would be raised again, and
the existing form of the human body be reproduced, the

---

[1] 2 *Cor.* 9 καὶ μὴ λεγέτω τις ὑμῶν
ὅτι αὕτη ἡ σὰρξ οὐ κρίνεται οὐδὲ
ἀνίσταται. γνῶτε· ἐν τίνι ἐσώθητε,
ἐν τίνι ἀνεβλέψατε, εἰ μὴ ἐν τῇ σαρκὶ
ταύτῃ ὄντες; δεῖ οὖν ἡμᾶς ὡς ναὸν
θεοῦ φυλάσσειν τὴν σάρκα· ὃν τρόπον
γὰρ ἐν τῇ σαρκὶ ἐκλήθητε, καὶ ἐν τῇ
σαρκὶ ἐλεύσεσθε...ἐν ταύτῃ τῇ σαρκὶ
ἀποληψόμεθα τὸν μισθόν.

[2] *sim.* v. 7, 2 βλέπε μήποτε ἀναβῇ
ἐπὶ τὴν καρδίαν σου τὴν σάρκα σου
ταύτην φθαρτὴν εἶναι καὶ παραχρήσῃ
αὐτῇ ἐν μιασμῷ τινι. ἐὰν γὰρ μιάνῃς
τὴν σάρκα σου, μιανεῖς καὶ τὸ πνεῦμα
τὸ ἅγιον· ἐὰν δὲ μιάνῃς τὴν σάρκα, οὐ
ζήσῃ.
[3] *de res. carn.* 63.

hands and feet and other members returning to their
old functions[1]. St Paul's illustration of the seed supplied, as he points out, a truer conception of the mystery.
But Origen's protest did not command the assent of
the great Church teachers of the following centuries.
It was combated by Methodius[2], and more hotly, *more
suo*, by Jerome. The words of the symbol were quoted
against it. "In your exposition of the Faith," writes
Jerome in his attack upon John of Jerusalem, "when
"you deal with the Resurrection, the word 'body' is
"used nine times, and 'flesh' not once." He anticipates
the reply that 'body' and 'flesh' mean the same thing,
but he does not admit its validity, and closes the controversy with an appeal to the Roman Creed, "which
"ends the whole mystery of Christian doctrine with the
"words *carnis resurrectionem*[3]." On this question Rufinus was at one with Jerome. His Creed accentuated its
confession of a resurrection of the flesh by prefixing
*huius* to *carnis*—possibly a relic of some early struggle of
the Aquileian Church with Docetic Gnosticism. Rufinus
interprets *huius carnis* as teaching the absolute identity

[1] Hieron. *ep.* 38 (*ad Pammach.*)
dicit Origenes in pluribus locis...
duplicem errorem uersari in ecclesia,
nostrorum et haereticorum; nos sim-
plices et φιλόσαρκας dicere quod
eadem ossa et sanguis et caro, id
est, uultus et membra totiusque
compago corporis resurgat in nouis-
sima die, scilicet ut pedibus ambu-
lemus, &c....est, inquit, singulis
seminibus ratio quaedam a Deo
artifice insita quae futuras materias
in medullae principiis tenet...sic et
in ratione humanorum corporum
manent quaedam surgendi antiqua
principia.
[2] In his treatise περὶ ἀναστάσεως,
of which fragments are preserved in

Epiph. *haer.* 64 and Phot. *bibl.* cod.
234.
[3] *L.c.* haec est omnis caussa cur in
expositione fidei tuae ad decipiendas
aures ignorantium nouies 'corpus'
et ne semel quidem 'carnem' nominas...scio enim te hoc esse dictu-
rum: Putaui idem corpus esse quod
carnem, simpliciter sum loquutus.
quare non carnem potius nominas,
ut corpus significes, et indifferenter
nunc carnem, nunc corpus?...in
symbolo fidei et spei nostrae...omne
Christiani dogmatis sacramentum
carnis resurrectione concluditur. et
tu in tantum in corporis et iterum
corporis...et usque nouies corporis
uel sermone uel numero immoreris.

of the future with the present body. To deny this seemed to him to be a reflexion on the power of God: "Why," he asks, "should we take so low a view of the "Divine omnipotence as to refuse to believe that God "can call together the scattered dust[1]?" The argument was felt to be a formidable one. Augustine in his early lecture *De fide et symbolo* ventures to say, "Illo tempore "immutationis angelicae non iam caro erit et sanguis, "sed tantum corpus...in caelestibus...nulla caro, sed "corpora simplicia et lucida quae adpellat Apostolus "*spiritualia*"; but in the *De ciuitate* (xxii. 20) he repeats and amplifies Rufinus's reference to the omnipotence of God, and in the *Retractations* he guards against his earlier words being understood as a denial of the prevalent belief[2]. Later Latin writers followed Augustine, the only important exception being the independent thinker of the ninth century, Johannes Scotus Erigena[3], whose philosophical mind rebelled against materialistic interpretations of the faith.

To return to the use of the phrase in the Creed. Its introduction into the Baptismal Creeds was doubtless the work of the age which was occupied in refuting Gnosticism. There is no reason to doubt that it had established itself in the Roman symbol by the middle of the second century. From Rome it passed to Carthage,

---

[1] *comm. in symb.* 42 cur, quaeso, tam angustus et inualidus diuinae potentiae aestimator es ut dispersam uniuscuiusque carnis puluerem in suam rationem colligi et reparari posse non credas?...et ideo satis caute fidem symboli ecclesia nostra docet quae in eo quod a ceteris traditur *carnis resurrectionem*, uno addito pronomine tradidit *huius c. r.* —huius sine dubio quam habet is qui profitetur, signaculo crucis fronti imposito.

[2] *retract.* i. 17 quisquis ea sic accipit ut existimet ita corpus terrenum quale nunc habemus in corpus caeleste resurrectione mutari ut nec membra ista nec carnis sit futura substantia, procul dubio corrigendus est, commonitus de corpore domini —an argument consistently employed by the advocates of an absolute reproduction of the existing form.

[3] *de diuin. nat.* iv. 12.

and to the Churches of Italy; no Western Creed abandoned it or modified it in any way if we except the
addition of the emphatic *huius* by the Church of Aquileia.
In the East, on the other hand, possibly through the
influence of Origen, a change set in during the fourth
century. Εἰς σαρκὸς ἀνάστασιν stood in the ancient
Creed of Jerusalem, and it appears in the Creed of the
*Apostolical Constitutions.* On the other hand the 'Con-
'stantinopolitan' Creed has προσδοκῶμεν ἀνάστασιν νεκρῶν, and Dr Hort notices that "σαρκός is absent from
"all known revised Eastern Creeds[1]." At the present
time the Orthodox, Armenian, and Nestorian Churches
of the East agree in confessing the 'resurrection of
'the dead[2],' while the whole Latin West preserves in the
Baptismal Creed the original *carnis resurrectionem.*

The Anglican Church possesses yet a third form of
words to express the same truth. With the rest of the
Western Church and the Orthodox Eastern Church she
acknowledges the "resurrection of the dead" in the
Creed of the Eucharist; with the unreformed Churches
of the West she retains the "resurrection of the flesh"
in the interrogative Creed of Baptism. But in the
Apostles' Creed of the daily offices she has substituted
'the resurrection of the body.' Perhaps the nearest
symbolical precedent for this phrase is to be found in
the *Quicunque:* "omnes homines resurgere habent cum
"corporibus suis." *Corporis* or *corporum resurrectio* was
open to suspicion in Jerome's time; it was thought to
savour of Origenism, if of nothing worse[3]. Our reformers,

[1] *Two Dissertations*, p. 91, *n.* 2;
conf. *ib.* p. 80.
[2] *Ib.* pp. 141, 146, 149.
[3] *ep.* 41 (*ad Pamm. et Ocean.*)
'Credimus (inquiunt) resurrectionem

futuram corporum.' hoc, si bene
dicatur, pura confessio est; sed...
corpus ponunt non carnem ut ortho-
doxus corpus audiens carnem putet,
haereticus spiritum recognoscat.

who were very far from entertaining heretical views upon the doctrine of the Resurrection, were probably attracted to the phrase by its Scriptural character; it appeared in the *Necessary Doctrine* of 1543, and when in 1552 the Creed was for the first time printed in full in the Order for Morning Prayer, it took a permanent place in the English Prayer-Book.

Thus in the English Church the old form of words, although not abandoned, is interpreted by a double gloss. The 'resurrection of the flesh' is retained as substantially equivalent to the 'resurrection of the dead' and to the 'resurrection of the body.' Yet the three forms are not mere synonyms. Each phrase has its own contribution to make to the fulness of the truth, while each needs to be guarded or supplemented by the other two. The 'resurrection of the dead' brings before the mind the vision of the general resurrection, at which "all that "are in the graves...shall come forth." The 'resurrection 'of the body' witnesses to the restoration of the individual life. The 'resurrection of the flesh' proclaims the continuity of the restored life with that which has gone before.

The tendencies of our own age are certainly not such as to encourage the Church to abandon the oldest of these symbolical forms. If in the second century the Gospel of the Resurrection was ridiculed by Pagan philosophy and frittered away by Christian heresy, there are forces at work in these last years of the nineteenth century which under other names and altered circumstances are tending to the same results. There is the same necessity for asserting in terms from which no ingenuity can escape the reality of the hope by which the Risen Lord has "brought life and immortality to light."

# APPENDIX.

Some forms of the Baptismal Creed and of other Creeds to which reference has been made in the foregoing pages are printed here for the convenience of readers who do not possess the collections of Hahn and Heurtley.

# A.

## WESTERN CREEDS.

### P. 9.

CREED OF THE PRYMER (cent. xiv.).
(Maskell, *Monumenta ritualia*, ii. 177.)

I bileue in god, fadir almy₃ti, makere of heuene and of erthe: and in iesu crist the sone of him, oure lord, oon aloone: which is conceyued of the hooli gost: born of marie maiden: suffride passioun undir pounce pilat: crucified, deed, and biried: he wente doun to hellis: the thridde day he roos a₃en fro deede: he stei₃ to heuenes: he sittith on the ri₃t syde of god the fadir almy₃ti: thenus he is to come for to deme the quyke and deede. I bileue in the hooli goost: feith of hooli chirche: communynge of seyntis: for₃yuenesse of synnes: a₃enrisyng of fleish, and euerlastynge lyf. so be it.

### CREED OF THE 'KING'S BOOK.'

I beleue in God the Father almighty, maker of heauen and earth; and in Iesu Christe, his only sonne our Lorde; whiche was conceiued by the Holy Goste, borne of the Virgine Mary, suffred under Ponce Pylate, was crucified, dead, buried, and descended into hell; and the third day he rose agen from deth; he ascended into heaven, and sitteth on the right hand of God the Father almighty; from thens he shall come to judge the quicke and the deade. I beleve in the Holy Goste; the holy Catholike Church; the communyon of sayntes; the forgyveness of synnes, the resurrection of the body; and the lyfe everlastynge. Amen.


### P. 10.

#### INTERROGATORY CREED OF THE GELASIAN SACRAMENTARY.

*Inde benedicto fonte baptizas unumquemque in ordine suo sub has interrogationes:*

Credis in Deum Patrem omnipotentem?

*Resp.* Credo.

Credis et in Iesum Christum Filium eius unicum, Dominum nostrum, natum et passum?

*Resp.* Credo.

Credis et in Spiritum Sanctum, sanctam ecclesiam, remissionem peccatorum, carnis resurrectionem?

*Resp.* Credo.


#### INTERROGATORY CREED OF THE SARUM *Ritus baptizandi.*

*Deinde interrogato nomine eius respondeant,* N. *Item sacerdos:*

N., credis in Deum Patrem omnipotentem, creatorem caeli et terrae?

*Resp.* Credo.

*Item sacerdos:* Credis et in Iesum Christum Filium eius unicum, Dominum nostrum, natum et passum?

*Resp.* Credo.

*Item sacerdos:* Credis et in Spiritum Sanctum, sanctam ecclesiam catholicam, sanctorum communionem, remissionem

peccatorum, carnis resurrectionem, et uitam aeternam post
mortem?

*Resp.* Credo.


## INTERROGATORY CREED OF THE FIRST ENGLISH BOOK OF COMMON PRAYER (1549).

*Then shall the Priest demand of the child...these questions
following, first naming the child, and saying:*

\*　　　\*　　　\*　　　\*

*Minister.* Dost thou believe in God the Father Almighty,
Maker of heaven and earth?

*Answer.* I believe.

*Minister.* Dost thou believe in Jesus Christ His only
begotten Son our Lord, and that He was conceived by the
Holy Ghost, &c....Dost thou believe this?

*Answer.* I believe.

*Minister.* Dost thou believe in the Holy Ghost, the holy
Catholic Church, &c.?

*Answer.* I believe.


## Pp. 11, 15.

## CREED OF PRIMINIUS († 758), WITH ITS LEGENDARY SETTING (cf. Caspari, *anecd.* p. 158 sq.).

Tunc ipsi discipuli domini reuersi sunt Hierosolyma, et
erant perseuerantes unanimiter in oratione usque ad decimum
diem quod est Pentecoste, et dicitur quinquagesimus dies
dominicus; et in ipsa die, hora tertia, factum est repente de
caelo sonus tanquam aduenientis spiritus uehementis et impleuit
totam domum ubi erant sedentes apostoli. et apparuerunt illis
dispertitae linguae tanquam ignis, seditque supra singulos
eorum et repleti sunt omnes Spiritu Sancto, et coeperunt loqui
aliis linguis prout Spiritus Sanctus dabat eloquii illis; et

composuerunt symbolum. Petrus: *Credo in Deum Patrem omnipotentem, creatorem caeli et terrae.* Iohannes: *Et in Iesum Christum*[1] *Filium eius unicum dominum nostrum.* Iacobus dixit: *Qui conceptus est de Spiritu Sancto, natus ex Maria uirgine.* Andreas ait: *Passus sub Pontio Pilato, crucifixus, mortuus et sepultus.* Philippus dixit: *Descendit ad inferna.* Thomas ait: *Tertia die surrexit a mortuis.* Bartolomaeus ait: *Ascendit ad caelos, sedit ad dexteram Dei Patris omnipotentis.* Matthaeus ait: *Inde uenturus iudicare uiuos et mortuos.* Iacobus Alphaei dixit: *Credo in Spiritu Sancto.* Simon Zelotes ait: *Sanctam ecclesiam catholicam*[2]. Iudas Iacobi dixit: *Sanctorum communionem, remissionem peccatorum.* Item Thomas ait: *Carnis resurrectionem*[3], *uitam aeternam.*

P. 13.

CREED OF THE BRITISH MUSEUM MS. ROYAL 2 A. XX.

Credo in Deum Patrem omnipotentem, et in Iesum Christum Filium eius unicum dominum nostrum, qui natus est de Spiritu Sancto et Maria uirgine, qui sub Pontio Pilato crucifixus est et sepultus, tertia die resurrexit a mortuis, ascendit in caelos, sedit ad dexteram Dei Patris, unde uenturus est iudicare uiuos ac mortuos. et in Spiritum Sanctum, sanctam ecclesiam catholicam, remissionem peccatorum, carnis resurrectionem. amen.

CREED OF THE BRITISH MUSEUM MS. GALBA A. XVIII.

Πιστεύω εἰς θεὸν πατέρα παντοκράτορα, καὶ εἰς Χριστὸν Ἰησοῦν υἱὸν αὐτοῦ τὸν μονογενῆ τὸν κύριον ἡμῶν, τὸν γεννηθέντα ἐκ πνεύματος ἁγίου καὶ Μαρίας τῆς παρθένου, τὸν ἐπὶ Ποντίου Πιλάτου σταυρωθέντα καὶ ταφέντα, τῇ τρίτῃ ἡμέρᾳ ἀναστάντα

---

[1] cod. *Iesu Christo.*     [2] cod. *ecclesia catholica.*
[3] cod. *ressurectione.*

ἐκ νεκρῶν, ἀναβάντα εἰς τοὺς οὐρανούς, καθήμενον ἐν δεξιᾷ τοῦ πατρός, ὅθεν ἔρχεται κρῖναι ζῶντας καὶ νεκρούς· καὶ εἰς πνεῦμα ἅγιον, ἁγί[αν ἐκκλησίαν], ἄφεσιν ἁμαρτιῶν, σαρκὸς ἀνάστα[σιν]. ἀμήν.

[The above is a transliteration from the Roman characters in which the Greek has been written by the scribe.]

CREED OF MARCELLUS (Epiph. *haer.* LXXII. 3).

Πιστεύω εἰς θεὸν παντοκράτορα, καὶ εἰς Χριστὸν Ἰησοῦν τὸν υἱὸν αὐτοῦ τὸν μονογενῆ τὸν κύριον ἡμῶν, τὸν γεννηθέντα ἐκ πνεύματος ἁγίου καὶ Μαρίας τῆς παρθένου, τὸν ἐπὶ Ποντίου Πιλάτου σταυρωθέντα καὶ ταφέντα καὶ τῇ τρίτῃ ἡμέρᾳ ἀναστάντα ἐκ τῶν νεκρῶν, ἀναβάντα εἰς τοὺς οὐρανοὺς καὶ καθήμενον ἐν δεξιᾷ τοῦ πατρός, ὅθεν ἔρχεται κρίνειν ζῶντας καὶ νεκρούς· καὶ εἰς τὸ ἅγιον πνεῦμα, ἁγίαν ἐκκλησίαν, ἄφεσιν ἁμαρτιῶν, σαρκὸς ἀνάστασιν, ζωὴν αἰώνιον.

P. 14.

CREED OF COD. LAUD. (Bodl. Gr. 35).

Credo in Deum Patrem omnipotentem; et in Christum Iesum[1] Filium eius unicum dominum nostrum, qui natus est de Spiritu Sancto et Maria uirgine, qui sub Pontio Pilato crucifixus est et sepultus, tertia die resurrexit a mortuis, ascendit in caelos[2], sedet ad dexteram[3] Patris, unde uenturus est iudicare uiuos et mortuos; et in Spiritu Sancto, sancta ecclesia, remissione peccatorum, carnis resurrectione[4].

[1] cod. x̄p̄o īh̄u.        [2] cod. *caelis.*        [3] cod. *dextera.*
[4] cod. *resurrectionis.*

## P. 15.

### CREED OF THE BANGOR ANTIPHONARY.

Credo in Deum Patrem omnipotentem, inuisibilem, omnium creaturarum uisibilium et inuisibilium conditorem. Credo et in Iesum Christum Filium eius unicum dominum nostrum, Deum omnipotentem, conceptum de Spiritu Sancto, natum de Maria uirgine, passum sub Pontio Pilato[1]; qui crucifixus et sepultus descendit[2] ad inferos, tertia die resurrexit a mortuis, ascendit in caelos[3] seditque ad dexteram Dei Patris omnipotentis, exinde uenturus[4] iudicare uiuos ac mortuos. Credo et in Spiritum Sanctum, Deum omnipotentem, unam habentem substantiam cum Patre et Filio ; sanctam esse ecclesiam[5] catholicam, abremissa[6] peccatorum, sanctorum communionem[7], carnis resurrectionem ; credo uitam post mortem et uitam aeternam in gloria Christi. Haec omnia credo in Deum. Amen.

## P. 22.

### CREED OF THE C. C. C. MS. 468 (saec. xv.).

Πιστεύω εἰς θεὸν πατέρα παντοκράτορα, ποιητὴν οὐρανοῦ καὶ γῆς· καὶ Ἰησοῦν Χριστὸν υἱὸν αὐτοῦ τὸν μονογενῆ τὸν κύριον ἡμῶν, τὸν συλληφθέντα ἐκ πνεύματος ἁγίου, γεννηθέντα ἐκ Μαρίας[8] τῆς[9] παρθένου, παθόντα ἐπὶ Ποντίου Πιλάτου, σταυρωθέντα, θανόντα[10], καὶ ταφέντα, κατελθόντα εἰς τὰ κατώτατα· τῇ τρίτῃ ἡμέρᾳ ἀναστάντα ἀπὸ τῶν νεκρῶν, ἀνελθόντα εἰς τοὺς οὐρανούς, καθιζόμενον ἐν δεξιᾷ θεοῦ πατρὸς παντοδυνάμου· ἐκεῖθεν ἐρχόμενον κρῖναι ζῶντας καὶ νεκρούς. πιστεύω εἰς τὸ πνεῦμα τὸ ἅγιον, ἁγίαν καθολικὴν ἐκκλησίαν, ἁγίων κοινωνίαν, ἄφεσιν ἁμαρτιῶν, σαρκὸς ἀνάστασιν, ζωὴν αἰώνιον. ἀμήν.

[The above is a transliteration from the Roman characters in which the Greek has been written by the scribe.]

---

[1] cod. *pylato*.   [2] cod. *discendit*.   [3] cod. *caelis*.   [4] cod. *uenturum*.
[5] cod. *aecclesiam*.   [6] cod. *abremisa*.   [7] cod. *commonionem*.
[8] cod. Μαρειας vid.   [9] cod. την vid.   [10] cod. θανεντα vid.

## P. 24.

### RULE OF FAITH ACCORDING TO TERTULLIAN.

#### *De praescr.* 13.

Regula est autem fidei...illa scilicet qua creditur unum omnino Deum esse...qui universa de nihilo produxerit per Verbum suum...Filium eius appellatum...delatum ex spiritu Patris Dei et uirtute in uirginem Mariam, carnem factum et in utero eius et ex ea natum exisse Iesum Christum...crucifixum tertia die resurrexisse, in caelos ereptum sedisse ad dexteram Patris, misisse uicariam uim Spiritus Sancti...uenturum cum claritate ad sumendos sanctos in uitae aeternae et promissorum caelestium fructum et ad profanos iudicandos igni perpetuo, facta utriusque partis resuscitatione cum carnis restitutione.

#### *De virg. vel.* 1.

Regula quidem fidei una omnino est...credendi scilicet in unicum Deum omnipotentem, mundi conditorem, et Filium eius Iesum Christum, natum ex virgine Maria, crucifixum sub Pontio Pilato, tertia die resuscitatum a mortuis, receptum in caelis, sedentem nunc ad dexteram Patris, uenturum iudicare uiuos et mortuos per carnis etiam resurrectionem.

#### *Adv. Prax.* i. 16.

Unicum quidem Deum credimus, sub hac tamen dispensatione...ut unici Dei sit et Filius...hunc missum a Patre in uirginem ex ea natum, hominem et Deum, filium hominis et Filium Dei, et cognominatum Iesum Christum ; hunc passum, hunc mortuum et sepultum...et resuscitatum a Patre, et in caelo resumptum sedere ad dexteram Patris, uenturum iudicare uiuos et mortuos ; qui exinde miserit secundum promissionem suam a Patre Spiritum Sanctum, Paracletum, sanctificatorem fidei eorum qui credunt in Patrem et Filium et Spiritum Sanctum.

### RULE OF FAITH ACCORDING TO NOVATIAN.

Regula exigit ueritatis ut primo omnium credamus in Deum
Patrem et Dominum omnipotentem...eadem regula ueritatis
docet nos credere post Patrem etiam in Filium Dei Christum
Iesum, Dominum Deum nostrum...sed enim ordo rationis
et fidei auctoritas...admonet nos post haec credere etiam
in Spiritum Sanctum.

### CREED OF NICETAS.

Credo in Deum Patrem omnipotentem, et in Filium eius
Iesum Christum, natum ex Spiritu Sancto et ex Maria uirgine,
sub Pontio Pilato passum crucifixum et mortuum.   Tertia die
resurrexit uiuus a mortuis, ascendit in caelos, sedet ad dexteram
Dei Patris, inde uenturus iudicare uiuos et mortuos.   Et in
Spiritum Sanctum, sanctam ecclesiam catholicam, communionem sanctorum, in remissionem peccatorum, huius carnis
resurrectionem, et in vitam aeternam.

### P. 61.

### CREED OF AQUILEIA (Rufin. *in symb.*).

Credo in Deo Patre omnipotente, inuisibili et impassibili ;
et in Christo Iesu, unico Filio eius domino nostro, qui natus
est de Spiritu Sancto ex Maria uirgine crucifixus sub Pontio
Pilato et sepultus descendit in inferna, tertia die resurrexit a
mortuis, ascendit in caelos, sedet ad dexteram Patris ; inde
uenturus est iudicare uiuos et mortuos.   et in Spiritu Sancto ;
sanctam ecclesiam, remissionem peccatorum, huius carnis
resurrectionem.

P. 62.

### CREED OF VENANTIUS FORTUNATUS.

Credo in Deum Patrem omnipotentem, et in Iesum Christum
unicum Filium, qui natus est de Spiritu Sancto ex Maria
uirgine, crucifixus sub Pontio Pilato, descendit ad infernum,
tertia die resurrexit, ascendit in caelum, sedet ad dexteram
Patris, iudicaturus uiuos et mortuos. Credo in Sancto Spiritu ;
sanctam ecclesiam, remissionem peccatorum, resurrectionem
carnis.

P. 84.

### CREED OF FAUSTUS OF RIEZ.

Credo in Deum Patrem omnipotentem, et in Filium eius
dominum nostrum Iesum Christum, qui conceptus est de
Spiritu Sancto, natus ex Maria uirgine, crucifixus et sepultus,
tertia die resurrexit, ascendit ad caelos, sedet ad dexteram Dei
Patris omnipotentis, inde uenturus iudicare uiuos et mortuos.
Credo in Spiritum Sanctum, sanctam ecclesiam catholicam,
sanctorum communionem, abremissionem peccatorum, carnis
resurrectionem, uitam aeternam.

B.

## EASTERN CREEDS.

### P. 38.

#### THE NICENE FAITH.

Πιστεύομεν εἰς ἕνα θεὸν πατέρα παντοκράτορα, πάντων ὁρατῶν τε καὶ ἀοράτων ποιητήν· καὶ εἰς ἕνα κύριον Ἰησοῦν Χριστόν, τὸν υἱὸν τοῦ θεοῦ, γεννηθέντα ἐκ τοῦ πατρὸς μονογενῆ, τουτέστιν ἐκ τῆς οὐσίας τοῦ πατρός, θεὸν ἐκ θεοῦ, φῶς ἐκ φωτός, θεὸν ἀληθινὸν ἐκ θεοῦ ἀληθινοῦ, γεννηθέντα οὐ ποιηθέντα, ὁμοούσιον τῷ πατρί, δι᾽ οὗ τὰ πάντα ἐγένετο τά τε ἐν τῷ οὐρανῷ καὶ τὰ ἐν τῇ γῇ· τὸν δι᾽ ἡμᾶς τοὺς ἀνθρώπους καὶ διὰ τὴν ἡμετέραν σωτηρίαν κατελθόντα καὶ σαρκωθέντα, ἐνανθρωπήσαντα, παθόντα, καὶ ἀναστάντα τῇ τρίτῃ ἡμέρᾳ, ἀνελθόντα εἰς οὐρανούς, καὶ ἐρχόμενον κρῖναι ζῶντας καὶ νεκρούς. καὶ εἰς τὸ ἅγιον πνεῦμα.

#### EARLY CREED OF JERUSALEM.

##### (Collected from Cyril.)

Πιστεύομεν εἰς ἕνα θεὸν πατέρα παντοκράτορα, ποιητὴν οὐρανοῦ καὶ γῆς, ὁρατῶν τε πάντων καὶ ἀοράτων· καὶ εἰς ἕνα κύριον Ἰησοῦν Χριστόν, τὸν υἱὸν τοῦ θεοῦ τὸν μονογενῆ, τὸν ἐκ τοῦ πατρὸς γεννηθέντα θεὸν ἀληθινὸν πρὸ πάντων τῶν αἰώνων, δι᾽ οὗ τὰ πάντα ἐγένετο· σαρκωθέντα καὶ ἐνανθρωπήσαντα, σταυρωθέντα καὶ ταφέντα, ἀναστάντα τῇ τρίτῃ ἡμέρᾳ, καὶ ἀνελθόντα εἰς τοὺς οὐρανούς, καὶ καθίσαντα ἐκ δεξιῶν τοῦ πατρός, καὶ ἐρχόμενον ἐν δόξῃ κρῖναι ζῶντας καὶ νεκρούς· οὗ τῆς βασιλείας οὐκ ἔσται τέλος. καὶ εἰς ἓν ἅγιον πνεῦμα, τὸν παράκλητον, τὸ λαλῆσαν ἐν τοῖς προφήταις· καὶ εἰς ἓν βάπτισμα μετανοίας εἰς ἄφεσιν ἁμαρτιῶν, καὶ εἰς μίαν ἁγίαν καθολικὴν ἐκκλησίαν, καὶ εἰς σαρκὸς ἀνάστασιν, καὶ εἰς ζωὴν αἰώνιον.

P. 97.

CREED OF THE APOSTOLICAL CONSTITUTIONS (vii. 41).

Μετὰ δὲ τὴν ἀποταγὴν συντασσόμενος [ὁ βαπτιζόμενος] λεγέτω ὅτι Καὶ συντάσσομαι τῷ χριστῷ· καὶ πιστεύω καὶ βαπτίζομαι εἰς ἕνα ἀγέννητον μόνον ἀληθινὸν θεὸν παντοκράτορα, τὸν πατέρα τοῦ χριστοῦ, κτίστην καὶ δημιουργὸν τῶν ἁπάντων, ἐξ οὗ τὰ πάντα· καὶ εἰς τὸν κύριον Ἰησοῦν τὸν χριστόν, τὸν μονογενῆ αὐτοῦ υἱόν, τὸν πρωτότοκον πάσης κτίσεως, τὸν πρὸ αἰώνων εὐδοκίᾳ τοῦ πατρὸς γεννηθέντα [οὐ κτισθέντα], δι᾽ οὗ τὰ πάντα ἐγένετο τὰ ἐν οὐρανοῖς καὶ ἐπὶ γῆς ὁρατά τε καὶ ἀόρατα, τὸν ἐπ᾽ ἐσχάτων τῶν ἡμερῶν κατελθόντα ἐξ οὐρανῶν καὶ σάρκα ἀναλαβόντα, ἐκ τῆς ἁγίας παρθένου Μαρίας γεννηθέντα, καὶ πολιτευσάμενον ὁσίως κατὰ τοὺς νόμους τοῦ θεοῦ καὶ πατρὸς αὐτοῦ, καὶ σταυρωθέντα ἐπὶ Ποντίου Πιλάτου καὶ ἀποθανόντα ὑπὲρ ἡμῶν, καὶ ἀναστάντα ἐκ τῶν νεκρῶν μετὰ τὸ παθεῖν τῇ τρίτῃ ἡμέρᾳ, καὶ ἀνελθόντα εἰς τοὺς οὐρανοὺς καὶ καθεσθέντα ἐν δεξιᾷ τοῦ πατρός, καὶ πάλιν ἐρχόμενον ἐπὶ συντελείᾳ τοῦ αἰῶνος μετὰ δόξης κρῖναι ζῶντας καὶ νεκρούς· οὗ τῆς βασιλείας οὐκ ἔσται τέλος. βαπτίζομαι καὶ εἰς τὸ πνεῦμα τὸ ἅγιον, τουτέστι τὸν παράκλητον, τὸ ἐνεργῆσαν ἐν πᾶσι τοῖς ἀπ᾽ αἰῶνος ἁγίοις, ὕστερον δὲ ἀποσταλὲν παρὰ τοῦ πατρός, κατὰ τὴν ἐπαγγελίαν τοῦ σωτῆρος ἡμῶν κυρίου Ἰησοῦ Χριστοῦ, καὶ μετὰ τοὺς ἀποστόλους δὲ πᾶσι τοῖς πιστεύουσιν ἐν τῇ ἁγίᾳ καθολικῇ καὶ ἀποστολικῇ ἐκκλησίᾳ· εἰς σαρκὸς ἀνάστασιν καὶ εἰς ἄφεσιν ἁμαρτιῶν καὶ εἰς βασιλείαν οὐρανῶν καὶ εἰς ζωὴν τοῦ μέλλοντος αἰῶνος.

## CREED OF CONSTANTINOPLE.

Πιστεύομεν εἰς ἕνα θεὸν πατέρα παντοκράτορα, ποιητὴν οὐρανοῦ καὶ γῆς, ὁρατῶν τε πάντων καὶ ἀοράτων· καὶ εἰς ἕνα κύριον Ἰησοῦν Χριστόν, τὸν υἱὸν τοῦ θεοῦ τὸν μονογενῆ, τὸν ἐκ τοῦ πατρὸς γεννηθέντα πρὸ πάντων τῶν αἰώνων, φῶς ἐκ φωτός, θεὸν ἀληθινὸν ἐκ θεοῦ ἀληθινοῦ, γεννηθέντα οὐ ποιηθέντα, ὁμοούσιον τῷ πατρί, δι' οὗ τὰ πάντα ἐγένετο· τὸν δι' ἡμᾶς τοὺς ἀνθρώπους καὶ διὰ τὴν ἡμετέραν σωτηρίαν κατελθόντα ἐκ τῶν οὐρανῶν, καὶ σαρκωθέντα ἐκ πνεύματος ἁγίου καὶ Μαρίας τῆς παρθένου καὶ ἐνανθρωπήσαντα, σταυρωθέντα τε ὑπὲρ ἡμῶν ἐπὶ Ποντίου Πιλάτου, καὶ παθόντα καὶ ταφέντα καὶ ἀναστάντα τῇ τρίτῃ ἡμέρᾳ κατὰ τὰς γραφάς, καὶ ἀνελθόντα εἰς τοὺς οὐρανοὺς καὶ καθεζόμενον ἐκ δεξιῶν τοῦ πατρός, καὶ πάλιν ἐρχόμενον μετὰ δόξης κρῖναι ζῶντας καὶ νεκρούς· οὗ τῆς βασιλείας οὐκ ἔσται τέλος. καὶ εἰς τὸ πνεῦμα τὸ ἅγιον τὸ κύριον τὸ ζωοποιόν, τὸ ἐκ τοῦ πατρὸς ἐκπορευόμενον, τὸ σὺν πατρὶ καὶ υἱῷ συμπροσκυνούμενον καὶ συνδοξαζόμενον, τὸ λαλῆσαν διὰ τῶν προφητῶν· εἰς μίαν ἁγίαν καθολικὴν καὶ ἀποστολικὴν ἐκκλησίαν. ὁμολογοῦμεν ἓν βάπτισμα εἰς ἄφεσιν ἁμαρτιῶν· προσδοκῶμεν ἀνάστασιν νεκρῶν, καὶ ζωὴν τοῦ μέλλοντος αἰῶνος. ἀμήν.

CAMBRIDGE: PRINTED BY J. AND C. F. CLAY, AT THE UNIVERSITY PRESS.

Made in the USA
Monee, IL
22 April 2022